THE
EVERYTHING®
BUDGETING
BOOK
2nd Edition

Dear Reader,

When my editor first approached me to write this book, I jumped at the chance. As a child, I spent every dime I made from babysitting and my paper route the moment I made it—and sometimes before. I believed then that the surest route to happiness was to spend, spend, spend. As I grew up, a few key mentors taught me the value of developing financial goals, saving, and paying off debts as early as possible. In short, I've come to the point where I've found that paying off debt is much more fun than getting into it.

I'm so pleased to offer you this second edition of *The Everything® Budgeting Book*. It contains all the helpful guidance from the first edition, as well as updates and new information. For example, I've added a chapter on budgeting for two (when moving in together and/or getting married) and a chapter on budgeting through a separation or divorce. I've now experienced both in my life, and this edition is far stronger with the addition of those two chapters. Plus, this second edition gave me the chance to update Web sites, government resources, and other outdated information. So, what you hold in your hands now is the latest and greatest way to budget your way toward your financial goals! I wish you all the best in your journey.

Tere Stouffer

Welcome to the EVERYTHING Series!

These handy, accessible books give you all you need to tackle a difficult project, gain a new hobby, comprehend a fascinating topic, prepare for an exam, or even brush up on something you learned back in school but have since forgotten.

You can choose to read an *Everything®* book from cover to cover or just pick out the information you want from our four useful boxes: e-questions, e-facts, e-alerts, e-ssentials. We give you everything you need to know on the subject, but throw in a lot of fun stuff along the way, too.

We now have more than 400 *Everything®* books in print, spanning such wide-ranging categories as weddings, pregnancy, cooking, music instruction, foreign language, crafts, pets, New Age, and so much more. When you're done reading them all, you can finally say you know *Everything®*!

QUESTION?

Answers to common questions

FACTS

Important snippets of information

ALERTS!

Urgent warnings

ESSENTIALS

Quick handy tips

DIRECTOR OF INNOVATION Paula Munier

EDITORIAL DIRECTOR Laura M. Daly

EXECUTIVE EDITOR, SERIES BOOKS Brielle K. Matson

ASSOCIATE COPY CHIEF Sheila Zwiebel

ACQUISITIONS EDITOR Lisa Laing

ASSOCIATE DEVELOPMENT EDITOR Katie McDonough

PRODUCTION EDITOR Casey Ebert

Visit the entire Everything® series at *www.everything.com*

THE
EVERYTHING®
BUDGETING BOOK

2nd Edition

Practical advice for spending less, increasing savings, and having more money for the things you really want

Tere Stouffer

Avon, Massachusetts

An Everything® Series Book.
Everything® and everything.com® are registered trademarks of F+W Media, Inc.

Published by Adams Media, a division of F+W Media, Inc.
57 Littlefield Street, Avon, MA 02322 U.S.A.
www.adamsmedia.com

ISBN 10: 1-59869-631-9
ISBN: 13: 978-1-59869-631-8

Printed in the United States of America.

J   I   H   G   F   E   D   C

Library of Congress Cataloging-in-Publication Data
is available from the publisher.

This publication is designed to provide accurate and authoritative information with regard to the subject matter covered. It is sold with the understanding that the publisher is not engaged in rendering legal, accounting, or other professional advice. If legal advice or other expert assistance is required, the services of a competent professional person should be sought.

—From a *Declaration of Principles* jointly adopted by a Committee of the American Bar Association and a Committee of Publishers and Associations

Many of the designations used by manufacturers and sellers to distinguish their products are claimed as trademarks. Where those designations appear in this book and Adams Media was aware of a trademark claim, the designations have been printed with initial capital letters.

This book is available at quantity discounts for bulk purchases.
For information, please call 1-800-289-0963.

To Maxie, who has her own small budget
(doggie day care, chew bones, lots and lots of food),
but deserves an even bigger one!

Contents

What Is Budgeting—and Why Do I Need to Do It? / 1

Prioritizing Your Spending / 13

Assessing Your Current Financial Situation / 33

Creating a Livable Budget / 45

Acknowledgments

Special thanks to the following for help with this book:

To the editors at Adams Media, including Jill Alexander and Lisa Laing, who believed I could share enough about my own budgeting experiences to fill an entire book on the subject.

To Mom and Dad, who taught me that being broke because you lived your dream isn't fatal—you can bounce back.

And to Grandma, who believed that being debt-free was the surest route to a happy life.

Top Ten Occasions to Rework Your Budget

1. When you start a new job, whether your income is higher or lower

2. When you move to a new house, buy a new car, or take on any other major expense

3. When an unexpected amount of money falls in your lap

4. When you suddenly have to spend an unexpected amount of money

5. When you have a baby, whether it's your first or your fourth

6. When your baby leaves the nest

7. When you get married

8. When you decide to end a marriage or other partnership

9. When you're thinking about starting a new business or retiring from your old one

10. When you have any new financial goal that you'd like to achieve

Introduction

▶ THIS BOOK IS CHOCK-FULL OF SOLID ADVICE—plus tips and tricks—to help you reach your financial goals, no matter what your current financial situation is and no matter how lofty your goals are. Okay, so you may not be able to cash out your stock portfolio and retire to Maui at age thirty-five, especially if you're currently thirty-four. But you can live a life free from the stress of dodging creditors and wondering how in the world you're going to make your rent or mortgage payment.

"How so?" you may ask. Well, imagine the following as your future life. Every two weeks, on a Friday, you receive a notice from your employer that your paycheck has been directly deposited to your bank: a portion to your retirement account, a portion to your savings account, and a portion to your checking account. During the weekend, you pay the bills that will come due before your next paycheck—and not only do you have enough money to cover all those bills, but you also withdraw some spending money for the next two weeks. Meanwhile, the money in your retirement account is increasing every day, and the money in your savings account—after the six months' salary you always leave in there for emergencies—is growing to pay for the sofa you've had your eye on, that vacation you're going to take next summer, the baby you're expecting later this year, or any other great use for your money you can think of!

Sound impossible? It's not. With careful budgeting—and a commitment to live within that budget—your life can be exactly like the one just described. Between now and then, though, you may have to radically rein in your spending, aggressively pay down your debts, and begin to save. If your situation is serious enough, you may have to live like a monk for the next six months (or more). But at the end of that time, you'll be well on your way toward developing a cushion of savings in the bank, planning for your retirement and/or your child's college education, and having enough income to meet your needs each month.

To get started, first you'll want to determine which part of your current spending plan is a high priority (see Chapter 2). Then you'll want to understand your overall financial picture, as it is now (see Chapter 3). Don't shy away from this step, even if you know that your financial picture is very, very bad. Knowing the full breadth of your assets and financial obligations helps you establish a budget (see Chapter 4) that will change your financial picture from bleak to promising.

If you're having trouble balancing your personal budget, consider putting a temporary moratorium on spending (see Chapter 5). You'll likely also want to cut down on your existing financial obligations, small and large (you can find all sorts of tips for doing this in Chapters 6, 7, and 8), immediately tackle your debt (Chapters 9 and 10), and, if necessary, find ways to add income so that you can get out of debt even faster (Chapter 11). Chapters 12, 13, and 14 help you live through unemployment and other budget catastrophes, including ways to get help from the government when necessary.

After that, you decide what other areas you need help with. Thinking about getting married or moving in with a partner? See Chapter 15. Worried about how to save for a new baby? Check out Chapter 16. Thinking about buying a house (and yes, you can save up enough for a down payment)? Visit Chapter 17. Are you saving for your child's education? See Chapter 18. Found yourself separated or divorced and aren't sure what financial step to take next? Turn to Chapter 19. Want to plan for retirement? See Chapters 20 and 21. Having trouble staying motivated? Use the ideas in Chapter 22.

Chapter 1

What Is Budgeting— and Why Do I Need to Do It?

Budgeting—the very word can bring tears to your eyes. Yet, if you've run into some financial difficulty and need to get back on track, budgeting is exactly the activity that will ultimately simplify and improve your life. This chapter tells you why and how.

Realizing What a Budget Is

Establishing a budget is the act of deciding how much of your money you're going to spend on one item, how much on another, and so on, before you're actually in the position of spending the money. Sticking to a budget is the act of following through on those decisions. Creating a budget isn't easy, but sticking to any budget is extremely difficult.

> You have to stick to the budget; the budget itself doesn't have the power to do that for you—it's just a piece of paper. Only you can decide that you're willing to stick to an uncomfortably low level of spending, work at another job to add income, or both.

The trick is to focus on the word *realistic*. It doesn't take much research or many difficult decisions to decide that you're going to spend $200 per month on food. But if you've never spent less than $500 per month on food, you'll blow your budget right out of the water the first week. Instead, before you begin deciding on the numbers in your budget, you'll need to fully assess your current situation, take a hard look at where you can cut back your financial obligations (both large and small), restructure your debt (if necessary), and see whether you can add income. Only then are you ready to decide realistically where every penny will be spent.

Recognizing What a Budget Isn't

A budget isn't a straitjacket that keeps you from really living. On the contrary, a budget that you stick to can be your ticket to living the life you imagine. Living within a strict budget isn't easy, but neither is being heavily in debt, worrying about how to pay for your expenses, and living with the guilt that goes with spending money you don't have. You've already done the hard part by living with financial insecurity; even though living within a budget isn't fun, it won't be any harder than that.

Keep in mind, though, that simply establishing a budget isn't the answer to your financial woes. Establishing even the world's greatest budget won't make any of your financial goals a reality unless you stick to the budget and follow through.

Understanding the Financial Goals

People establish budgets because they have financial goals that are not being met. They may not realize that they have any goals at all—they may just be tired of bill collectors calling—but everyone who establishes a budget has at least one unmet financial goal. For example, you may want to:

- Be able to pay all your bills from your paycheck—and maybe have a little left over
- Buy your first house
- Save for retirement, but can't seem to find any extra money to get started
- Pay off all your credit cards and never get into debt again
- Give more money to your church or to other nonprofits
- Be your own boss, but are nervous about not having money in the bank
- Take a vacation
- Stop hearing from the hospital about your medical bills
- Buy a new—or at least newer—car
- Stay home with your baby
- Remodel part of your house
- Pay for laser eye surgery
- Finance at least part of your child's college education
- Buy medical insurance
- Rebuild your credit
- Find a way to care for your aging parents
- Finally build your dream house
- Take a leave of absence from your job to work in the Peace Corps
- Go back to school and begin a new career

- Buy the downtown coffee shop when the current owners retire
- Get a whole new wardrobe

Are any of these your goals? If so, budgeting will get you there, even if the odds seem impossible right now. Even if you're stuck in a job you don't like, desperately want to go back to school, have to take care of an aging parent, and have $19,000 in credit card debt, you can meet your financial goals—just as others have done before you. With a good budget, a little patience, and a whole lot of determination, you'll eventually get there.

Not convinced that you need a budget? Here's a test to determine whether you need one: Do you have even one unmet financial goal? (See the preceding section for ideas.) As long as it's important to you, from wanting to put a decent meal on the table for your family to wanting to buy a great dress for your high school reunion to simply wanting to see a credit card bill that says your balance is $0, no goal is too big or too small. And if you're having trouble reaching your goal, you need a budget. Period.

Looking at a Sample Budget

Meet Billie DeSantos, age thirty-eight, whose budget we're going to peek at to see how this process works. Billie has worked at the same company for eight years, working up to management level last year. She bought a condominium six years ago, has a car payment on a three-year-old car, owes about $2,800 in credit card debt, has some money in savings, is a single parent with two kids (ages ten and fourteen), and participates in the company's 401(k) retirement plan. Billie usually has enough money to pay the bills every two weeks, although the kids' growing expenses are starting to pressure the family's income.

Sample Financial Goals

The first step in developing a budget is to decide what you want your finances to allow you to do in life (see the final section in this chapter). To this end, Billie has the following goals:

Help the kids pay for college. Pay for half the expenses at one of the three large state universities (currently $14,500 per year for tuition, fees, room, and board) or put that same amount toward a private or out-of-state college.

Pay off the credit card in nine months. Get the balance to zero, and then if it's used at all, pay it off in full every month.

Retire from the company at age fifty (in twelve years) and open a bed-and-breakfast in a small coastal town. B&Bs in similar towns currently cost about $650,000 for the building and operation, but that price will surely rise in twelve years.

Put away six months of income in a savings account over the next twelve years. This money would be for emergencies only, not to be touched for any other expenses.

Sample Income

Billie's biweekly income after taxes (which provides her with a refund of about $450 per year), company-sponsored medical and dental insurance (at a cost of $55 per pay period), company-sponsored life insurance for $250,000 of coverage ($30 per pay period), and 401(k) contributions ($75 per pay period, matched by the company) is $1,892, which totals $4,100 per month. Billie also has $1,700 in savings.

ESSENTIAL

How do you envision your retirement? For most people, retirement doesn't mean an endless vacation, but it does mean doing more of what you love: Switching to part-time work at your current job, taking up a new career, starting a business, babysitting your grandchildren, or building your dream house.

Sample Expenses

Monthly expenses are as follows (see Chapter 3 for details on how to total your own expenses):

Mortgage on the condo (30 years at 7.85%) includes taxes and insurance	$1,492
Car payment (4 years at 5.9%)	$342
Utilities	$375
Food (including eating out)	$675
Toiletries/haircuts	$85
Spending money/allowances	$200
Car maintenance/insurance/expenses ($1,600/year)	$133
Vacations ($2,800/year)	$233
Clothing ($3,200/year)	$267
Gifts and contributions	$200
Credit card debt ($2,800)	$50
TOTAL	$4,052

Remember to use these numbers only as a sample. If yours are much higher or much lower, that may be perfectly okay. Your situation is unique, and no one else's budgeting numbers should mean a whole lot to you.

Sample Ways to Reduce Debt

Billie's monthly obligations equal her monthly income, so to achieve her financial goals, some expenses must be eliminated (see Chapters 5 through 10). Here's what Billie decides to do:

Keep the car and car payment. After paying off the car in one year, continue to drive it for five years after that, putting $342 into savings each month for the next car. No monthly savings.

Cut down on utilities, such as getting rid of her land line (going cell-only) and installing a programmable thermostat (at cost of $46) to save on gas bill. Estimated monthly savings: $83.

Spend a maximum of $125 per week on groceries. Limit eating out to pizza or Thai takeout once a week. Estimated monthly savings: $175.

Eliminate the small stuff. Keep Starbucks visits to once per week, borrow magazines and DVDs from the library, and otherwise reduce monthly spending money to $150 ($100 for both kids' allowances; $50 for Billie). Monthly savings: $50.

Investigate car insurance options to lower annual insurance costs by $400. Monthly savings: $33.

Limit vacation spending to $500 per year by being creative (see Chapter 7). Monthly savings: $60.

Allow each member of the family $600 per year to spend on clothing and shoes (teaching the kids budgeting skills in the process). Any more than that, and the kids will have to use their allowances or get part-time jobs. Monthly savings: $117.

TOTAL Monthly Savings: $518

Meeting Goals for This Sample

Billie must increase monthly savings and investments to meet her financial goals:

Refinance the mortgage on the condo at 5.8% for fifteen years, paying it off in twelve (so that it can be sold, debt-free, to help pay for the B&B, which will then be mortgaged for fifteen years). Monthly increase: $290.

Use savings plus increase in monthly payment to pay off credit card in nine months. Monthly increase: $122.

Begin saving for college in Section 529 fund (see Chapter 18). Monthly new expense: $600.

Put away a safety net of six months of income over the next twelve years. Monthly new expense: $170.

TOTAL monthly increase: $1,182

Revisiting the Sample Goals and Priorities

Billie is $664 short each month, so it's time to revisit the listed goals to see which can be changed or eliminated. Here's the revised list of goals:

- Help the kids pay for college.
- Pay off the credit card in three months, and begin saving for the kids' college fund only when it's paid off.
- Retire from the company at age fifty-four (in sixteen years) and open a bed-and-breakfast in a small coastal town.
- Put away six months of income in a savings account over the next sixteen years.

QUESTION?

How many times should I adjust my budget?
Keep adjusting until your income exceeds your projected expenses (including money going into savings, retirement accounts, and so on). Until your financial obligations—including your financial goals—have been whittled down to fit your income, you don't really have a budget.

These changes mean the following financial adjustments:

Refinance the mortgage on the condo at 6 percent for thirty years, with the understanding that in eight years (when college savings will no longer be necessary), the money currently used to save for college will be redirected to the mortgage. Making those large extra payments toward the mortgage after the kids finish college will result in the mortgage being paid off in eighteen years, not thirty. Reduces monthly shortfall by $310.

Put away $130 per month into savings (instead of $170) over the next eight years, and then increase savings with reduction in food, utilities, clothing, and other expenses because the kids will have left home. Reduces monthly shortfall by $50.

Delay section 529 college fund by three months, using that money plus funds from savings to pay off credit card debt. After credit card is paid off, begin saving for college in Section 529 fund, putting $418 (instead of $600) away, with the understanding that all future promotions, raises, and tax refunds for the next eight years will go directly to the college savings account. Reduces monthly shortfall by $304.

TOTAL monthly increase from current spending: $0

Billie has created a working budget. It won't be easy to cut back, but the family does still have some discretionary spending money, the kids' educational savings are in good shape, and Billie will realize the dream of owning a B&B in just sixteen years.

Thinking about Your Long-Term Financial Goals

The first step in your own budgeting process is to think about your financial priorities and goals.

Deciding What's Important to You

A lot of people wish they could meet their financial goals in the future and still live well in the present. You may wonder why you can't retire at forty-five, and until then, still eat out every day, live in a luxurious house, and lease a BMW. After all, your neighbors live in a large house, drive expensive cars, eat at nice restaurants, wear tailored clothing, send their kids to private colleges, and have a boat—they don't appear to be giving up anything. Perhaps they're not, and they're much wealthier than you thought. Or (and this is more likely), they are drowning in debt, aren't working toward any financial goals, and aren't doing nearly as well as you think.

Keep in mind that you can live quite well in the United States without really having the means to do so. You can buy a house with very little money down and (for luxurious homes) stretch out the payments for as long as fifty years. You can lease a luxury automobile without having any intention of owning it. You can borrow money to pay for your kids' college educations. You can buy clothes and boats, take vacations, and eat in fine restaurants using credit cards, paying the money back very, very slowly. When your credit card bills get too high, you can borrow against the equity in your house to pay them off, or you can open up new credit card accounts. This is the way many Americans live—on borrowed money.

But at some point, it all catches up with people, and they either realize they're in deep financial trouble and must do something to get out, or they declare bankruptcy and spend ten or fifteen years fighting to rebuild their creditworthiness and reputation. Still others do nothing about their debt before they die, and their relatives spend years paying back the deceased person's financial obligations.

Only you can decide what's important to you. Don't let advertisements, your friends and coworkers, or your desire to keep up with the neighbors affect your priorities. You probably can't afford everything you want to buy and still reach your long-term financial goals, but you can feel satisfied if you're spending a little money now on the things that are most important to you and still working toward something bigger in the future.

Since you are reading this book, you've decided you no longer want to live that way, even if it is the way that so many other Americans live. Instead, you're willing to give up something now to have your financial goals met in the future. Exactly what you give up, though, is strictly up to you; you decide which expenses are most important right now. You may decide, for example, that life is too short to cut back on vacations, or that instead of spending time cooking, you want to be able to eat out every day and spend that time socializing with your family instead. That's perfectly okay. But in the process, you may, for example, also decide to sell your car or move to a much smaller house.

Don't think you can have it all because, chances are, you can't. But you can retain what's important to you while giving up what's much less important.

Making Your Financial Goals a Reality

Do you want to be debt-free? Do you want to pay for your child's college education? Do you want to retire comfortably at age sixty-five, or at age forty-five? This section helps you decide and understand what you'll have to do to make those goals a reality.

Your financial goals drive your budget and give you a reason to stick to it. Without written goals that every decision-maker in your household agrees to, you'll have a difficult time resisting spending money whenever the urge strikes.

Use **WORKSHEET 1-1** to write down all the financial goals you can think of. Whether you have just one goal or you end up with too many to fit on this worksheet, you're doing just fine. (For now, ignore the "Monthly Amount" and "Priority" columns.)

WORKSHEET 1-1

Your Financial Goals

Goal	Date	Amount Needed	Monthly Amount	Priority (1–5)
		$	$	
		$	$	
		$	$	
		$	$	
		$	$	
		$	$	
		$	$	
		$	$	

Now go back and assign a priority to each financial goal, with the numbers five through one meaning something like the following:

5. You would be miserable if you didn't achieve this financial goal by the proposed date.
4. You'd be very disappointed if you came to the end of your life and hadn't achieved this financial goal.

3. You would have some regrets if you didn't achieve this financial goal, but it wouldn't bother you for long.

2. While this goal is important, you have others that are far more important.

1. This is a fun goal to think about, but you're not really committed to it.

The reality is that you may not have enough income, or you may have too many expenses that you can't cut to meet all of your financial goals. With a prioritized list, however, you can decide which goals you want to attack right now and which ones can wait.

You have just one more step, and that's to turn your financial goals into monthly amounts. Simply divide the total amount needed by the number of months between now and your goal's due date. For a goal that you want to complete two years from now, for example, divide the amount of money needed by twenty-four to get the monthly amount.

ESSENTIAL

If you're married or otherwise have a decision-making partner in your finances, each of you should fill out Worksheet 1-1 independently, assigning your own priorities, and then share your worksheets with each other. You'll have to compromise on some goals and you may have to sit down several times to work out the details, but ultimately you'll emerge with shared financial goals that you can both look forward to.

Because you'll earn interest on your savings during that twenty-four months, you'll actually have a bit more than the amount needed, but because some savings accounts earn less than 2 percent interest, just keep it simple by forgetting about interest for now. (Chapter 21 tells you more about ways to earn more than standard interest rates.)

Chapter 2
Prioritizing Your Spending

This chapter helps you discover how much you spend every day and which of those expenses are important to you. You'll also find out how to stop spending altogether—a temporary situation, but a good technique to use when your spending is out of control. (Chapters 5, 6, and 7 also help you figure out how to spend less, every day.)

Why Not Spending Is the Key to Budgeting

You have two ways to free up money for your financial goals: Making more or spending less. Neither one is better than the other, right? Wrong! If 18 percent of your income goes to state and federal taxes, then for every extra dollar you earn, you can use only eighty-two cents to pay off debt or save for the future. But if you can save $1 of your expenses, you can apply all of it to your debt or put it into savings or investments.

Find out whether your employer offers direct deposit, a feature in which your check is deposited immediately into your bank account. Instead of a check, you receive a notice from your employer that the deposit has been made. You're more likely to save than spend if you use this feature.

Totaling Your Daily Expenses

The method of totaling your expenses in **WORKSHEETS** 2-1 through 2-7 is simple: You either report what you spent last week—day by day, expense by expense—or you start fresh this week and record every expenditure going forward. If you record your expenses this coming week, be sure you don't try to be "good" and spend less than you usually do.

You want to record every expense that you pay out-of-pocket, even the tiniest amounts. (If you happen to pay your monthly or biweekly bills on one of these seven days, do not record those payments here, you'll do that in the following section.)

WORKSHEET 2-1

Daily Expense Sheet: Monday

Item	Amount	Item	Amount
	$		$
	$		$
	$		$
	$		$
	$		$
	$		$
	$		$
	$		$
TOTAL:	$		$

WORKSHEET 2-2

Daily Expense Sheet: Tuesday

Item	Amount	Item	Amount
	$		$
	$		$
	$		$
	$		$
	$		$
	$		$
	$		$
	$		$
TOTAL:	$		$

WORKSHEET 2-3
Daily Expense Sheet: Wednesday

Item	Amount	Item	Amount
	$		$
	$		$
	$		$
	$		$
	$		$
	$		$
	$		$
	$		$
TOTAL:	$		$

WORKSHEET 2-4
Daily Expense Sheet: Thursday

Item	Amount	Item	Amount
	$		$
	$		$
	$		$
	$		$
	$		$
	$		$
	$		$
	$		$
TOTAL:	$		$

WORKSHEET 2-5
Daily Expense Sheet: Friday

Item	Amount	Item	Amount
	$		$
	$		$
	$		$
	$		$
	$		$
	$		$
	$		$
	$		$
TOTAL:	$		$

WORKSHEET 2-6
Daily Expense Sheet: Saturday

Item	Amount	Item	Amount
	$		$
	$		$
	$		$
	$		$
	$		$
	$		$
	$		$
	$		$
TOTAL:	$		$

WORKSHEET 2-7

Daily Expense Sheet: Sunday

Item	Amount	Item	Amount
	$		$
	$		$
	$		$
	$		$
	$		$
	$		$
	$		$
TOTAL:	$		$

Categorizing and Prioritizing Your Daily Expenses

Now, review your daily lists and categorize them in the most logical way you can: coffee, breakfasts, newspapers, lunches, DVD rentals, clothing, toiletries, groceries, and so on. Use **WORKSHEET 2-8** to record your findings. Ignore the "Priority" column until you've listed all of your expenses by category.

WORKSHEET 2-8

Daily Expense Summary

Category	Total Amount	Priority (1–5)
	$	
	$	
	$	
	$	
	$	
	$	
TOTAL:	$	

Now go back and assign a priority to each category—5 being something you absolutely can't live without, and 1 meaning you'd barely notice if you no longer spent money on this one. Your priorities don't necessarily mean that you will continue to spend this money in the exact same way.

Assessing Your Monthly Expenses

Recording your monthly expenses in **WORKSHEETS** 2-9 through 2-20 works just like your daily ones, except that while daily expenses are often cash expenditures that you may not really notice, monthly expenses such as rent and utilities are more likely to be paid by check or electronic transfer. For these monthly worksheets, you'll want to go back through your receipts, checkbook register, and bank statements, and also use your memory. If, on the other hand, you simply record all your monthly expenses starting in January, you'll understand your January expenses on January 31, but you won't have a clear picture of your December spending until a year from now, and that's valuable time that you could use to reach your financial goals instead of getting deeper into debt. Instead, to more quickly get a clear picture of your monthly expense, dig out your bank statements, checkbook register, receipts, and so on.

Be sure not to double up on daily and monthly expenses. If you've already recorded a certain expense on your daily expense sheets, do not record it here.

WORKSHEET 2-9
Monthly Expense Sheet: January

Date	Item	Amount
		$
		$
		$
		$
		$
		$
		$
		$
		$
		$
		$
		$
		$
		$
		$
		$
		$
		$
		$
		$
		$
		$
		$
TOTAL:		$

WORKSHEET 2-10
Monthly Expense Sheet: February

Date	Item	Amount
		$
		$
		$
		$
		$
		$
		$
		$
		$
		$
		$
		$
		$
		$
		$
		$
		$
		$
		$
		$
		$
		$
		$
		$
TOTAL:		$

WORKSHEET 2-11
Monthly Expense Sheet: March

Date	Item	Amount
		$
		$
		$
		$
		$
		$
		$
		$
		$
		$
		$
		$
		$
		$
		$
		$
		$
		$
		$
		$
		$
		$
		$
		$
TOTAL:		$

WORKSHEET 2-12
Monthly Expense Sheet: April

Date	Item	Amount
		$
		$
		$
		$
		$
		$
		$
		$
		$
		$
		$
		$
		$
		$
		$
		$
		$
		$
		$
		$
		$
		$
		$
TOTAL:		$

WORKSHEET 2-13
Monthly Expense Sheet: May

Date	Item	Amount
		$
		$
		$
		$
		$
		$
		$
		$
		$
		$
		$
		$
		$
		$
		$
		$
		$
		$
		$
		$
		$
		$
		$
TOTAL:		$

WORKSHEET 2-14
Monthly Expense Sheet: June

Date	Item	Amount
		$
		$
		$
		$
		$
		$
		$
		$
		$
		$
		$
		$
		$
		$
		$
		$
		$
		$
		$
		$
		$
		$
		$
TOTAL:		$

WORKSHEET 2-15
Monthly Expense Sheet: July

Date	Item	Amount
		$
		$
		$
		$
		$
		$
		$
		$
		$
		$
		$
		$
		$
		$
		$
		$
		$
		$
		$
		$
		$
		$
		$
TOTAL:		$

WORKSHEET 2-16
Monthly Expense Sheet: August

Date	Item	Amount
		$
		$
		$
		$
		$
		$
		$
		$
		$
		$
		$
		$
		$
		$
		$
		$
		$
		$
		$
		$
		$
		$
		$
		$
TOTAL:		$

WORKSHEET 2-17
Monthly Expense Sheet: September

Date	Item	Amount
		$
		$
		$
		$
		$
		$
		$
		$
		$
		$
		$
		$
		$
		$
		$
		$
		$
		$
		$
		$
		$
		$
		$
		$
TOTAL:		$

WORKSHEET 2-18
Monthly Expense Sheet: October

Date	Item	Amount
		$
		$
		$
		$
		$
		$
		$
		$
		$
		$
		$
		$
		$
		$
		$
		$
		$
		$
		$
		$
		$
		$
		$
TOTAL:		$

WORKSHEET 2-19
Monthly Expense Sheet: November

Date	Item	Amount
		$
		$
		$
		$
		$
		$
		$
		$
		$
		$
		$
		$
		$
		$
		$
		$
		$
		$
		$
		$
		$
		$
		$
TOTAL:		$

WORKSHEET 2-20
Monthly Expense Sheet: December

Date	Item	Amount
		$
		$
		$
		$
		$
		$
		$
		$
		$
		$
		$
		$
		$
		$
		$
		$
		$
		$
		$
		$
		$
		$
		$
		$
TOTAL:		$

Categorizing and Prioritizing Your Monthly Expenses

In the same way that you worked with the daily worksheets, group your monthly expenses into categories (utilities, rent, insurance) and add them to **WORKSHEET 2-8.** Then prioritize those categories (just as you did for your daily expenses).

ALERT!

Don't let once-in-a-while expenses catch you off guard! To be sure you've thought of everything, go through last year's checkbook, bank statements, receipts, or calendar to jog your memory about what you spent money on.

Prioritizing Which Items You Want to Spend Money On

You should now have a list of your expenses by category, with a priority attached to each one. If you have enough income to reach all of your financial goals and still spend money the way you currently do, you won't need this prioritized list, though it's likely you can't meet your financial goals if you continue to spend. Use this list to choose the areas that you absolutely do not want to cut back on (these are the items that have a priority rating of 5). If you have too many items with a high priority to meet your financial goals, subprioritize those items so that you come up with just a few. Spending on these items will make all the cutbacks easier to swallow.

Keep in mind that you are the only one who can determine your priorities. If you would rather drive an old car so that you can still afford to buy organic fruits and vegetables, do it.

Chapter 3

Assessing Your Current Financial Situation

In order to establish a budget, you have to understand your financial situation right now. That way, you can see exactly how far you have to go before you'll reach your goals. This chapter gives you worksheets and tips for identifying your financial goals, your income (money coming in to you), and your financial obligations (outflows of money).

Understanding Why Your Financial Situation Is Important

Before you can create a budget, you have to know every detail of your financial situation. Although you probably understand in general how much you spend and where you spend it, you may be amazed at how much you actually spend on certain items that don't seem like they could add up so fast.

The exercises and worksheets in this chapter are designed to give you an unflinchingly honest appraisal of where you stand. If you have a tendency to become overwhelmed easily, keep a friend on standby who you can phone for support, and keep upbeat music playing in the background as you put together your income and expenses.

Determining Your Income and Other Assets

Your income includes any money that comes into your possession and can be counted on in the near future. Your paycheck is considered income, but income isn't limited to a paycheck you receive from your employer, it is also a disability payment, a welfare check, a Social Security check, alimony, child support, self-employment income from a small business, and so on. Whatever money comes in—money that you can count on—is what you want to consider as income.

Keep in mind that income is considered income only if you can count on it. So getting lucky at the horse track this weekend is not income—because you could just as easily lose the same amount of money at the track.

Determine How Often You're Paid

First, determine how often you're paid at work:

- **Weekly:** Common for temporary and contract work
- **Biweekly:** The most common way companies pay their employees—usually every other Friday
- **Semimonthly:** Often paid on the first and fifteenth of each month
- **Monthly:** One paycheck each month
- **Quarterly:** Four times a year—this is rare
- **Semiannually:** Twice a year—this is also rare
- **Annually:** Almost unheard of unless you're on a board of directors

If you're paid on commission and aren't exactly sure when your next check will be coming, review your income from last year and use that as a starting point. If, however, something has changed since last year that may cause you to make fewer sales this year, adjust accordingly.

If you get paid monthly, you may have a harder time than most with your budget. The amount of your check may seem like a lot at the beginning of the month, but three or four weeks later, your expenses may have exceeded that check. A strict weekly budget can really help.

Identifying All Your Sources of Income

WORKSHEET 3-1 helps you identify all your sources of income, add them up, and figure them on an annual basis. In this worksheet, you calculate all of your income for a given pay period and multiply it to get an annual amount. Be sure to write down the net amount of each paycheck—that's the amount you take home after the taxes, insurance, union dues, and other items are deducted.

Don't overestimate your income or underestimate your expenses. The purpose of assessing your financial situation is so you'll have a real picture of your financial health, so you can start to improve it. If you fudge the numbers, you'll never be able to change your spending patterns.

WORKSHEET 3-1

Your Income and Assets

Weekly or Biweekly Sources of Income	Amount	Multiply by	Annual Amount
Weekly paycheck	$	52	$
Biweekly paycheck	$	26	$

Semimonthly Sources of Income	Amount	Multiply by	Annual Amount
Semimonthly paycheck	$	24	$

Monthly Sources of Income	Amount	Multiply by	Annual Amount
Monthly paycheck	$	24	$
Welfare check	$	24	$
Disability check	$	24	$
Social Security check	$	24	$

Quarterly Sources of Income	Amount	Multiply by	Annual Amount
Quarterly paycheck	$	4	$
Quarterly dividend from stocks	$	4	$

Semiannual Sources of Income	Amount	Multiply by	Annual Amount
Semiannual paycheck	$	2	$

Annual Sources of Income	Amount	Multiply by	Annual Amount
Annual paycheck	$	24	$

Other Sources of Income	Amount	Multiply by	Annual Amount
Alimony	$	12	$
Child support	$	12	$
TOTAL:	$		$

Remember that this is not projected income. Don't write down the income you *think* you'll have after a promotion or other situation; what you want to look at is exactly how much money you have to work with right now.

Calculating Your Financial Obligations: Debts and Living Expenses

In this section, you look at the debt and living expenses that you must pay (or, in some cases, choose to pay) each year. These range from your monthly rent or mortgage payment to a car payment or lease, utility bills (including your cell), food, entertainment, contributions to charities, gifts (holidays, weddings, birthdays), alimony payments, credit card payments, and store charge-card payments.

Don't try to be "good" when listing your current expenses. Base your list on what you've done in the past, not what you'd like to do in the future. If you've spent $150 each of the last five years at the January white sale, you may not be able to break that habit cold turkey.

Writing Down Full Debt Amounts

In **WORKSHEET 3-2,** indicate the *total amount* you owe on credit cards and store charge cards, don't write only the minimum payments. Here's why: Suppose you owe $5,000 to a credit card company, but rather than saying that you owe them $5,000 this month, your bill says that you have to make a payment of $65. That's your monthly payment, right? Wrong. Credit card and store charge-card companies are in the business of making money, and one way is by having you pay a high rate of interest on your debt for as long as possible. Did you know that if you make the minimum monthly payment, you might be paying on that $5,000 for ten or fifteen years? And that's without charging even one more item to your account in all that time! Paying the minimum is never going to help you get your financial situation under control. (You'll find ways to pay off this debt much more quickly in Chapters 9 and 10.)

Remember that "obligations" refer to any money you owe anyone. You may think your Grandma has forgotten all about that $5,000 she loaned you to buy a car, but write it down anyway. Grandma may have a better memory than you think!

Gathering Information

In order to fill out **WORKSHEET 3-2** (pages 40–41), you'll have to gather some information. You probably know how much your rent or mortgage payment is off the top of your head, but you may not know exactly how much your utility bills have been. To find that information, look back through your checkbook or receipts. If you can't come up with the amount, give your utility company a call. If you ask, they'll probably send you free copies of your bills for the last year.

Averaging Out Utility Payments

It's important to look at all of your utility payments—not just the one for last month—because some of them might change from month to month. For example, your electric bill may get much higher in the summer if you live in an area where air conditioning is critical to your comfort. Likewise, your gas bill may rise sharply in the winter if you live in an area that has low temperatures at that time of year. On the other hand, your water, cable, sewer, phone, and other utilities may not change at all.

To figure out how much your average electric bill is, add up your last twelve monthly payments to the electric company and divide by twelve. This will give you the average amount that you pay each month.

Remembering Periodic Expenses

Remember to consider the expenses that people tend to forget because they come due only every six or twelve months:

- Auto insurance
- Vehicle excise tax (if your state has one)
- Car repair and maintenance
- Homeowner's or renter's insurance
- Property taxes
- House repair and maintenance
- Gifts (holiday, birthday, wedding)
- Events to attend (such as weddings)
- Vacations

Unlike the income worksheet, for this worksheet, *do* try to anticipate any expense that may come up in the next twelve months, for you and your family. If your best friend who lives 2,000 miles away is probably going to get married, calculate the cost of that trip, the clothes you'll need, the gift you'll buy, and so on.

If, as part of your monthly mortgage payment, you pay one-sixth or one-twelfth of your homeowner's insurance and property taxes, which are then stored in an escrow account until they are due, write down your total monthly mortgage payment but do not include an amount on the lines that ask for your homeowner's insurance and property taxes.

If you'd find it easier to figure these expenses month by month, flip to Chapter 2 for twelve monthly worksheets for determining exactly when and how you spend your money.

WORKSHEET 3-2

Your Debt and Other Obligations

Weekly Obligations	Amount	Multiply by	Annual Amount
Groceries and household items	$	52	$
Day care	$	52	$
Contributions to church or other	$	52	$
Weekly rent on furniture or appliances	$	52	$
Entertainment/babysitting	$	52	$
Eating out, including coffee and lunch	$	52	$

Monthly Obligations	Amount	Multiply by	Annual Amount
Rent or mortgage	$	12	$
Car payment or lease	$	12	$
Electric bill (average)	$	12	$
Gas bill (average)	$	12	$
Water bill	$	12	$
Sewer bill	$	12	$
Trash-pickup bill	$	12	$
Cable/DSL/satellite bill	$	12	$
Telephone bill	$	12	$
Cell-phone bill	$	12	$
Bank charges (debit card, fees, etc.)	$	12	$
Haircuts/manicures/pedicures	$	12	$
Home equity loan	$	12	$
Other loan	$	12	$
Credit card or store-charge bill (total due)	$	12	$
Child support or alimony payment	$	12	$

WORKSHEET 3-2

Your Debt and Other Obligation (*continued*)

Quarterly Expenses	Amount	Multiply by	Annual Amount
Car maintenance	$	4	$
House maintenance	$	4	$

Semiannual Expenses	Amount	Multiply by	Annual Amount
Auto insurance	$	2	$
Property taxes	$	2	$
Wedding gifts	$	2	$
Events to attend	$	2	$
Clothing and shoes	$	2	$

Annual Expenses	Amount	Multiply by	Annual Amount
Homeowner's or renter's insurance	$	1	$
Vehicle registration and excise tax	$	1	$
Car repair	$	1	$
House repair and maintenance	$	1	$
Holiday gifts	$	1	$
Birthday gifts	$	1	$
Vacation	$	1	$
Club memberships	$	1	$

Other Expenses	Amount	Multiply by	Annual Amount
	$	_____	$
	$	_____	$
	$	_____	$
	$	_____	$
	$	_____	$
TOTAL:	$		$

Putting Income and Financial Obligations Together

The worksheet in this section is one of the most important tools for pinpointing why any financial troubles exist for you. In **WORKSHEET 3-3,** you combine information from **WORKSHEETS 3-1** and **3-2** (see the two preceding sections), and find out whether you have more obligations than income (which means you're probably in or close to being in debt), or if you have more income than obligations (which is the first step toward a healthier financial picture).

WORKSHEET 3-3
Your Income-to-Obligations Ratio

Your annual income (from Worksheet 3-1)		$
Your annual obligations (from Worksheet 3-2)	–	$
Your net income (may be a negative number)	=	$
Your annual income	÷	$
	×	100
Your income-to-obligations ratio (may be a negative number)	=	$

After you've completed **WORKSHEET 3-3,** let's assess how you did.

Ten or Greater: Your Income Far Exceeds Your Debts

Assuming you were honest in your assessment of your income and obligations, you should have no trouble establishing a budget you can live with. If you can't seem to come up with enough money to pay the bills each month or your credit card debts are growing, check out Chapter 2 to find tools for tracking your daily, weekly, and monthly expenses to get a handle on where your money is going.

Zero to Nine: Your Income Just Barely Exceeds Your Debts

What this means is that, on an annual basis, you just barely get by. If you have trouble paying your bills each month, you may have one of two problems. Either your expenses are actually higher than you think (see Chapter 2 for ways to track your expenses accurately), or you may have cash-flow problems (discussed in the following section).

Negative One to Negative Ten: Your Debt Just Barely Exceeds Your Income

Many people are living just a little above their means. In order to do this, they use credit cards, store charge cards, home equity loans, short-term loans, and so on to make ends meet. The problem is that if you're short $300 per month and use credit cards to pay for groceries or clothing, at the end of the year, you'll be $3,600 in debt. Ten years later, even with a credit card that gives you a decent interest rate, you'll be over $83,000 in debt!

Negative Ten or Less: Your Debt Far Exceeds Your Income

This situation often occurs during in-between times in life. For example, when you're in college or have just graduated but can't find a job, you're in between living off your parents and working full time to pay your own expenses, but you may still have the same spending patterns that you had when your parents were paying all your expenses. You may also have a lot of debt due to a layoff or medical leave, or when you have one huge debt hanging over your head, such as a school loan or unexpected medical bill.

FACT

The major reason people get into debt is that they spend more than they earn. Simple, right? Well, not really. For most people, income is fixed—you know how much your paycheck will be. But expenses can vary greatly, depending on, for example, how often you eat out, whether you update your wardrobe, and how many long-distance calls you make.

If you have more obligations than income, you're not alone. The average U.S. household has nearly $10,000 in credit card debt, which means that millions of Americans are likely to be in this exact situation, using credit cards as a way to keep up with expenses. If you find yourself with more obligations than income, see Chapter 8. That chapter gives you ideas for paring down some of those obligations so you have enough income to pay your bills every month.

Identifying Potential Cash-Flow Problems

Often, if your income just barely exceeds your obligations, on paper you look like you'll get by just fine, but in reality you may find yourself coming up short at certain times of the year.

Suppose, for example, that you have an income of $26,000 per year (after taxes) and $25,000 in obligations. A problem often arises when one of your periodic expenses, such as car insurance, is due. Technically, you might have enough income from January to December to cover your car insurance, but if your insurance bill arrives in February, you may not have had time to put enough money into savings each month to cover this expense. This is called a *cash-flow problem,* and in order to manage this situation successfully, you have to reduce your debt (or increase your income) to the point where you're living far enough below your income that you don't have trouble paying your large periodic expenses. See Chapters 5 through 10 for debt-reduction ideas and Chapter 11 for tips on increasing your income.

Taking a Break if You Need It

If your financial picture is rather bleak, this chapter may have been difficult for you. Chapter 4, which shows you how to establish a written budget that you're going to be living with for the next few months and years, probably isn't going to be any easier. Even if you're the type who likes to plow through one chapter to the next, you might want to take a break for a few hours or overnight. Don't give up here, though! Just take a short break, inhale deeply, and get ready to change your life for the better.

Chapter 4

Creating a Livable Budget

This chapter will help you create—and then evaluate the potential problems with—your first budget. You'll find out what elements are required for living a budgeted life, and then you'll work on your own budget with a detailed worksheet.

4

Making Your Financial Goals a Reality

The reason you create a budget is because you have financial goals. These may range from eliminating debt due to medical bills to saving for retirement to buying your first house. No matter what your financial situation, you have financial goals, even though you may not think of them that way. If you have a particular lifestyle you want to live, places you want to go, or people you want to help, you have financial goals.

Chapter 1 gives you a sample listing of a wide range of financial goals. Your list may be very different, and should be unique to your distinct set of circumstances. Whatever goals you have, they're right. No one else's goals are appropriate for you, and your set of goals probably isn't right for anyone else.

When you create a budget, you keep all of your financial goals as the central focus, figuring out how to cut your current expenses—or increase your current income—to get you on track to meet those goals. How you decide to cut back or add income will be as unique as your goals are. You may make very different choices than your neighbors do about how, how well, and where you'll live. Every decision you make will be specific to your financial goals and your current financial situation, which no one else has to know about or agree with. Just smile when people question your decisions, knowing you have quite a secret!

FACT

The secret to financial security is really quite simple. Spend less than you earn, save for the big-ticket items you have your eye on, keep money in the bank for emergencies, and plan for the day when you won't want to—or won't be able to—work as much.

Keep in mind, though, that you may not be able to meet every one of your goals if you also want to maintain your current level of spending. For more information, see Chapter 1 to decide which goals are most important to you and Chapter 2 to figure out how to prioritize your current expenses.

Spending Less Than You Make

To stay above water financially, you have to spend less than you make. This simple point is the most important principle for constructing and living within a budget. You simply cannot meet financial goals if you don't live within your means.

Most millionaires don't lead wild and exciting lives. They are ordinary folks who save a lot, are thrifty, and account for every penny. You, too, can amass a small fortune by renting DVDs instead of paying full price for movies, using coupons, skipping the daily Starbucks fix, turning down the thermostat, buying long-lasting clothing and shoes, and so on.

Yet many Americans spend more than they make, and it often starts with just a few bad decisions. Here's an example. A few years ago, a financial advisor on television said that as long as interest rates on new cars stayed at 0 or 1 percent (which car companies were offering at that time), the best financial investment a person could make would be to buy a new car. In fact, the person suggested that you'd have to be crazy not to take advantage of this situation. Hmm, suppose a person watching that program owned a five-year-old car that was completely paid off and ran fine; but hearing that financial advice, our car owner decided to go out and buy a new car. After all, the opportunity for financing this low might never come again. So, the car owner trades in the perfectly fine car and gets a great deal on a new car, but two months later, the car owner begins to feel the pinch. Monthly car payments went from $0 to $318, and insurance costs went up $168 per year. Before, our car-buying friend always had a bit of extra money every month—enough to put $200 in savings and still have a little left over. But now, there's nothing to go into savings and no extra cash around. In fact, even in the first few months, the car owner is beginning to put a few groceries on the credit card just to get by. Before long, this one innocent purchase has led to a spiraling financial problem.

The car was definitely not the best investment our car owner could have made. A far better decision would have been not to even think about getting a new car until the old one had a problem. The drop in interest rates saved our car owner money, but the car itself—at that particular time—was something our friend didn't need or plan for.

Remember: A product is only a good deal if you've planned for it and can afford it within the context of your other financial goals. Nothing—not low interest rates, a sale on shoes, the house of your dreams—is ever a good deal if it requires you to spend more than you make.

Spending Money Only on Budgeted Items

After you set up a budget, you can spend money only on the items that your budget says you can spend money on, and this drives most people crazy! They feel as though someone else is controlling their lives, or that they're living in a straitjacket. But, while budgets can be constricting, the only person controlling your spending is you—or, to be more exact, your financial goals.

Suppose your primary financial goal is to take a two-month trip to Europe. You're sure that you want to do this, and your budget reflects it. Because you'll be taking the time off work without pay, you're saving not only for the trip but also for the income you'll miss while you're gone. You've figured out that if you give up your biscotti and coffee every morning, turn down your thermostat, and stop buying clothes for a year, you'll be able to do it. But a couple of months into the year, you decide that this "crazy" budget isn't going to tell you how to run your life and that no one should live without biscotti and coffee in a not-very-warm house while wearing old clothes.

What exactly has happened here? Basically, your financial goals have a higher priority than wanting to go to Europe. So, the budget has to be reworked to reflect those financial goals, because if biscotti and clothes aren't in the budget, you can't spend money on them and still make it to Europe. In order to spend euros a year from now, you can't buy items now that you've agreed to give up.

Saving for Unexpected Expenses

People often get into financial trouble because they don't expect the unexpected. By intentionally saving for unexpected expenses, you can break this cycle. An unexpected expense may be an auto accident that requires you to pay your deductible or a repair to your home. An emergency can even be a planned expense that comes due before you expect it. For example, suppose you had planned to take a vacation later this year, but your best friend is attending a conference in the Bahamas and asks you to go along, stay for free in the hotel, and pay only airfare and food. You might decide that now is a better time to take an inexpensive vacation. However, given your goal to get out and stay out of debt, you don't dare put the trip on credit cards. This trip will be a much easier decision for you if you have money in the bank to borrow against.

Make sure that you have an allotment for savings in your budget, even if it's just $10 per paycheck for now, and work toward eventually saving up to six months' salary for every wage earner in your household.

Ideally, you should keep six months' income in the bank. If there are two wage earners in your family, keep six months of each person's income in savings. Yes, this is a lot of money, but if you're able to save this much money, you have choices in your life. You're never going feel stuck again: If you're laid off, you have time to find a job you really want; if you've been looking for a new house and find the perfect one, but the current owners won't wait for you to sell yours first, you can use your savings as a down payment, replacing the savings after you sell your existing house.

The trick to having money available for unexpected expenses is twofold. First, you never dip into your savings unless you're faced with a truly unique situation. A shoe sale at your favorite department store is not a unique situation. And if you have time to plan for an unexpected event, save in advance by changing your lifestyle to free up more money for savings, but don't dip into your savings unless you absolutely have to. The money in your savings account is for that oh-my-gosh-what-am-I-going-to-do-now situation.

The second part of the trick to keeping savings on hand for unexpected events is always to replace it after you use it. If you have six months' salary in the bank and you use one month's salary to make up the difference between your disability pay and your normal pay, when you get back to work full time, immediately begin replacing that one month's salary.

These two concepts—leaving money in savings for unexpected expenses and replacing any money that you borrow from your savings when unexpected situations arise—are not common in our society. You'll find that the majority of Americans don't think they're capable of doing this. If they see they have money in the bank, they'll spend it on whatever they think will make their lives better at that moment. But the truth is, having this security gives you the power to choose, and that's the greatest power you'll ever have—much greater than the big-screen TV for the Super Bowl.

Revisiting Your Goals and Priorities

As you go through the budgeting process, you may find yourself revising your long-term financial goals and your shorter-term spending priorities. This revising doesn't make you a bad person! It's just the reality of everyone's situation: We each have a set income, and our desires to spend exceed our income.

Suppose, for example, that you have the following goals: Save for a small down payment on a house in six months; buy new furniture for your house when you move in; and within two years, increase savings so that it equals six months' worth of income. You also have your eye on buying a new car in a year, and you've recently added this to your list of goals. Suppose that with your current income, you spend everything you make. Well, in order to save $10,000 for a down payment on a house in six months, you're going to need to save roughly $1,500 per month. The furniture is going to cost $500 for six months, saving six months' salary is going to require $900 a month for two years, and the new car, minus the trade-in on your existing car, will take $1,200 a month for a year. Altogether, this is $4,100 a month. Unless you're currently living an incredibly lavish lifestyle, the chance of being able to cut $4,100 out of your current spending to find this money is slim.

You have two options. You can find a way to make more money by getting a second job, doing freelance work, starting your own part-time business, working overtime, or finding a new job that pays more money (see Chapter 11 for more information). That is one way to meet your goals, but keep in mind that whenever you work more hours, you give up something very precious—time. If you have the time to spend, if you are planning to work the extra hours only for a short while, and if working more hours isn't going to jeopardize your health, wreak havoc on your relationship with your kids or spouse, or take you away from a hobby that you love, perhaps it will be okay. But if you have to commit to this lifestyle for ten years, you may find it unacceptable.

QUESTION?

Isn't re-evaluating the same thing as selling out?
Not at all. Re-evaluating isn't unusual and doesn't mean you've sold out. Instead, it's the only way to generate a budget that will actually work for you in the long term.

The other option is to go back and revisit your spending priorities and financial goals. Even if you've cut your expenses as much as you think you can, maybe you can still cut back some more. Even if one of your spending priorities is to be able to talk on the phone for an unlimited amount of time with long-distance friends and relatives, perhaps you could talk during free weekend minutes or switch to e-mail part of the time. Or you may decide that because your financial goals are very important, you're willing to give up this expense, even if you've previously decided that it was a high priority.

On the other hand, you may decide to re-evaluate your goals, to look for changes there. Perhaps, for example, you decide to buy the house in four years instead of six months, which gives you much more time to save for the down payment and the furniture. Perhaps, because both the house and the phone calls are important enough, you can make do with your existing car for several more years. Perhaps you keep working toward getting six months' salary in the bank, but stretch that goal out to ten years instead of two.

Generating a Budget You Can Stick To

This section walks you through the steps for generating your own budget.

Starting with Your Goals

If you haven't yet written down your goals, you must start there. See Chapter 1 for a worksheet that will help you generate your long-term financial goals, and then return here. You'll need to know your goals before you can establish a budget.

ESSENTIAL

To be useful, your goals must be in financial terms, with actual dollar amounts attached, and must have set deadlines attached to them. Otherwise, what you call goals are really only pipe dreams.

Looking at which Expenses You're Willing to Cut

If you haven't yet looked at all of your expenses and decided which are priority items that you want to keep in your budget, first take a look at Chapter 2. Come back here when you're done.

Knowing Your Income

Before you can establish a budget, you have to know exactly how much money you have coming in every month from your employer after taxes, union dues, medical insurance, 401 (k) contributions, and so on. Chapter 3 helps you track all this information. If you haven't already done this, go there before coming back to this section to work on your budget.

Getting Started

To make your first stab at a budget, simply fill out **WORKSHEET** 4-1.

WORKSHEET 4-1
Your First Budget

Monthly income (or annual income divided by 12)	$
Monthly financial obligations	– $
Monthly amount needed to meet goals	– $
Balance (may be a negative number)	= $

Checking the Balance

If the balance in **WORKSHEET** 4-1 is a positive number, you're done! You've established a budget for yourself that, while perhaps not easy to stick to, will certainly be doable.

If, however, the balance is a negative number, you have an unbalanced budget and need to look again at your goals, expenses, and income. (You may want to use a pencil for the worksheets in the two following sections in case you have to revise them again, and again, and again!)

Revisiting Your Goals

Now's the time to go back through your goals from Chapter 1 and rework them if you can. Wherever possible, change the amount of time or money needed, starting with your lowest-priority items. **WORKSHEET** 4-2 can help.

Taking a Harder Look at Your Expenses

Another way to balance your budget is to look more closely at your expenses. Worksheet 4-3 helps you think through expenses you can cut further (use the worksheets in Chapter 2 to help you establish priorities). Chapters 5 through 8 give you concrete suggestions for ways to cut back on your spending.

WORKSHEET 4-2
Reworking Your Goals

Goal	Date	Amount Needed	Monthly Amount	Priority (1–5)
		$	$	
		$	$	
		$	$	
		$	$	
		$	$	
		$	$	
		$	$	
		$	$	

WORKSHEET 4-3
Reworking Your Monthly Expenses

Monthly Expense	Amount	Ways to Reduce	New Amount
Groceries and household items	$		$
Day care	$		$
Contributions	$		$
Savings	$		$
Rent on furniture or appliances	$		$
Entertainment/babysitting	$		$
Eating out	$		$
Rent or mortgage	$		$
Car payment or lease	$		$
Electric bill (average)	$		$
Gas bill (average)	$		$
Sewer bill	$		$
Water bill	$		$
Trash pick-up bill	$		$

WORKSHEET 4-3

Reworking Your Monthly Expenses (*continued*)

Monthly Expense	Amount	Ways to Reduce	New Amount
Cable/DSL/satellite bill	$		$
Telephone bill	$		$
Cell phone bill	$		$
Bank charges	$		$
Haircuts/manicures/pedicures	$		$
Home equity loan	$		$
Other loan	$		$
Credit card or store-charge bill	$		$
Credit card or store-charge bill	$		$
Credit card or store-charge bill	$		$
Credit card or store-charge bill	$		$
Child support or alimony	$		$
Car maintenance	$		$
House maintenance	$		$
Auto insurance	$		$
Property taxes	$		$
Gifts	$		$
Events to attend	$		$
Clothing and shoes	$		$
Home insurance	$		$
Vehicle registration	$		$
Vacation	$		$
Club membership	$		$
Club membership	$		$
TOTAL:	$		$

Deciding Whether You Can Increase Your Income

A final way to balance your budget is to find ways to increase your income. See Chapter 11 to brainstorm additional ways to find more money. Be sure, however, that these opportunities for added income are actually in the bag—don't count on "possible" income when budgeting.

Taking a Second Stab at a Budget

With revised goals and a new spending plan, you're ready for version two of your budget. See **WORKSHEET 4-4.**

WORKSHEET 4-4
Version Two of Your Budget

Monthly income		$
Monthly financial obligations	−	$
Monthly amount needed to meet goals	−	$
Balance (may be a negative number)	=	$

Checking the Balance—Again

If your balance is now positive, you're done! Congratulations on working through your first budget. Chances are, though, that it's still negative, and you'll have to continue this process through many renditions. Start again: Revisit your goals, look at your expenses, and decide whether you can increase your income.

Don't get discouraged by all this revising—this is the essence of budgeting. If the process were easy, that is, if you could come up with a workable budget on your first try, people wouldn't have trouble living with budgets.

Continuing this Process Until You Have a Budget

WORKSHEET *4-5* gives you another chance to work through a budget, but do this one in pencil because you'll probably need to work through the numbers again. Keep going until the budget is completely balanced, and one you're able to live with. The key words in this section are "able to live with." Never forget that you are going to live with this budget every hour of every day until the day you meet your financial goals. If you don't think you can do that, revise your budget again!

WORKSHEET 4-5
Version Three of Your Budget

Monthly income	$
Monthly financial obligations	– $
Monthly amount needed to meet goals	– $
Balance (may be a negative number)	= $

Chapter 5

Freezing Your Spending for the Short Term

If your spending is getting the best of you and creating more and more debt for your family, try freezing your spending for the next several months. Freezing your spending isn't easy, but it can stop your accelerating debt dead in its tracks.

What Freezing Really Means

Freezing means going cold turkey on your spending—you temporarily stop buying. For the short term, you cut out all but the most essential spending; your cuts will include personal appliances, home appliances, clothing, shoes, CDs, DVDs, decorative items, linens, computer accessories, and so on. You freeze your spending for a predetermined amount of time—usually six to twelve months—and just stop shopping. Of course, you can still buy groceries and the required supplies for your home, but you don't buy anything else.

FACT

Some people believe that they must spend in order to keep the American economy going. While consumer spending does impact how much money many businesses make, your six or nine months of thriftiness is not going to spin the economy into an uncontrolled recession. Besides, you'll be back someday.

Reducing Temptation During a Freeze

People who temporarily freeze their spending usually find that the best way to stay the course is to steer clear of opportunities to spend money:

- Don't read the ads that come in the Sunday paper.
- Don't stop at outlet malls when you travel.
- Dispose of all the catalogs you have in your possession.
- Call all the companies that send you catalogs and have them both remove your name from their mailing lists and stop selling your name to other companies.
- Don't visit Internet sites that sell products.
- Don't go to the shopping-mall food court for a quick meal.
- Don't meet friends for an afternoon at the mall or any other store.
- Don't go window shopping at an appliance, music, or computer store.

- Discontinue any music or book clubs, even if you have to buy your remaining required purchases to do so.
- When grocery shopping, don't inadvertently wander into the consumer-goods section of the store.
- Send gift certificates instead of actual purchases as gifts, so that you don't have to go to a store or browse a catalog or Web site.

The following sections will help you freeze your spending a little less painfully.

Establishing What's Really a Need

Understanding the difference between a need and a want is really the crux of sorting out your financial difficulties. In an effort to make ourselves feel better about being consumers, we continually elevate wants to the level of needs. But we actually have few needs, at least in the realm of products that you can buy:

- Shelter
- Clothing
- Food and water

Thousands of years ago, this list meant a mud, straw, or wooden hut, along with some animal skins and just enough calories to survive. Today, we have escalated these basic human needs, and they have become so intertwined with wants that we're not sure how to separate them. Yes, you need shelter, but you do not need a four-bedroom home with a formal dining room, a fireplace in the great room, a three-car garage, a kitchen with cherry cabinets, and a bonus room over the garage. That's a want.

The same is true for clothing. Humans need a way to stay warm and dry, but they do not need ten suits or eight pairs of jeans. Those are wants. And while everyone needs food and water to survive, that food does not have to come from a five-star restaurant. You also only need enough calories to survive, not enough to add three to five pounds each year, as the average American does.

The desire to own and consume is very strong in Americans, and it enables us to justify nearly any purchase in the name of needs. Don't buy into it. Instead, use **WORKSHEET 5-1** to list every need you have (you might want to use a pencil, though, and keep a good eraser handy). Be very specific in your list: Don't just list "house"; instead, write a description of the house you need and the amount it will cost.

WORKSHEET 5-1
Needs Versus Wants

Need (Description)	Cost	Consequences of Not Buying
	$	
	$	
	$	
	$	
	$	
	$	
	$	
	$	
	$	

Identifying the Consequences of Not Meeting a Need

After you've listed all your needs, identify what would happen to you if you didn't get each one, asking yourself the following questions:

- Would you or others around you die?
- Would you or others suffer physical pain or extreme physical discomfort?
- Would your health or the health of others suffer in the long term?
- Do you know for sure that you would lose your job without this item?

If none of these would happen, it isn't a need, it's a want, and you have no business buying it during a spending freeze. Remember this the next time your mind tries to talk your wallet into giving in.

Establishing—and Sticking to—a Shopping List for Your Needs

Before you leave the house and head out to spend money, write out a shopping list of your needs (which are likely to include only groceries and toiletries). Be sure that they're needs, and don't pad the list because you're in the mood to buy. Keep in mind that you are probably feeling deprived, so you may try to satisfy your spending itch by splurging on groceries and toiletries.

Before you leave for the store, write down everything you need to get, and also scribble in an estimate of how much each item will cost. Then total the bill. If it's less than you planned to spend, stop writing out your list and immediately go to the store. If the total is more than you planned to spend, begin crossing items off your list before you go, until you get down to the budgeted amount.

ALERT!

Don't justify veering from the list because something is "such a good deal." Instead, remember that the best possible deal is to spend $0, so even if an item is half price, you can't buy it unless it's on your list.

Then, buy only the items on the list. Don't add items to the list and then cross them off while you're standing in the checkout lane. Instead, stick absolutely to your list. If you see something you're sure you need but it isn't on your list, put it on next week's list when you get home. Today, you can buy only what's on your list. Be vigilant about this process, and you'll never overspend on groceries and toiletries again.

Putting Away Your Credit Cards

No, seriously, put them away for at least six months. Put them in a safe place that's hard to get to, such as a safe-deposit box at the bank (which will probably cost around $20 per year, an amount that's worth spending if it keeps you from getting further into debt). The farther away the credit cards are from you, the better.

For six months, pay for all of your day-to-day purchases with cash and pay your bills with a check. When you're shopping for purchases that are allowed—such as groceries and toiletries—write out a list before you go, estimate how much you'll need, and take no more than $10 over that amount. When you're not supposed to be making any purchases, limit the amount of cash you carry around to $5 and a few quarters. That will allow you to pay for parking if you need to, but not lunch or a flat-screen TV!

Tucking Away Your Debit Card

Although a debit card is technically like cash or a check, in reality it feels much more like a credit card. Because you don't hand over cash, you may feel as though you're not really paying for this purchase, much like when you use a credit card. And if those funds are earmarked for other needs (like paying off your debt or saving for a vacation), you'll end up without enough money to meet your needs by the end of the month.

If you take $80 in cash to the grocery store, you'll be very careful not to exceed that amount with convenience foods. But if you take a debit card, you're not likely to be nearly as careful. Put the debit card in the same place you put the credit cards—your best bet is in a safe-deposit box.

Creating a Wish List

A wish list is an outlet for your hot little fingers and creative mind while you're in a spending freeze. The basic idea is that you write down everything you'd ever like to buy. The list may range from a new TV to whitening strips for your teeth to a sailboat. Anything you're not allowed to buy during a spending freeze is fair game. Nothing on the list has to be sensible or practical or a wise financial decision.

Sometimes when you're not spending, you feel disconnected from our consumer-oriented society, and a wish list makes you feel like your old self again. When you feel the itch to spend, go online or look at a friend's catalogs and write down the item number, description, page number, and so on of any item that looks interesting. Act as if you're really going to buy the item. But don't. Just add the item to your list and let the list sit for a while. The act of writing the item down will feel, strangely enough, very similar to how you feel when you actually buy something. It sounds completely crazy, but it works! (See Chapter 22 for additional tips on how to survive a spending freeze.)

ESSENTIAL

When you brainstorm your wish list, think pie-in-the-sky. You're just daydreaming right now—later, you can make your list more realistic. So write down whatever you can imagine in your future. But make sure it's your wish list. Don't put a sailboat on your list if you really don't like water!

Paring Down the Wish List

Just listing the items can be cathartic when you want to buy, buy, buy. But listing the items on **WORKSHEET 5-2** can also help you cross some items off the list. When you write down an item's name and cost, also check off one of the three needs categories: "Need Today," "Need This Month," or "Would Like Someday." If none applies, don't check anything off. Tomorrow, revisit any item that you indicated you needed today. Is the need still strong? In a month, review any items that you needed this month, and also look at the items that you'd like someday. Do you still feel strongly about them? Cross off any item you no longer feel you need and/or check off new categories for some items.

WORKSHEET 5-2

Your Wish List

Item Name	Cost	Need Today?	Need This Month?	Would Like Someday?
	$			
	$			
	$			
	$			
	$			
	$			
	$			
	$			
	$			
	$			
	$			
	$			
	$			
	$			
	$			
	$			
	$			
	$			
	$			
	$			

Reviewing a Sample Wish List

Your wish list may look like **TABLE 5-3:**

TABLE 5-3

Sample Wish List

Item Name	Cost	Need Today?	Need This Month?	Would Like Someday?
Smoothie maker	$30		✓	
Honda Element	$26,000			✓
Garden arbor	$275			✓
New luggage	$350			✓
Two pairs of jeans	$130	✓		
iPod	$249			✓
Cabin in the woods	$210,000		✓	

Now, suppose thirty days have gone by, and the list looks like **TABLE 5-4**:

TABLE 5-4

Sample Wish List, Round Two

Item Name	Cost	Need Today?	Need This Month?	Would Like Someday?
Smoothie maker	$30		✓	
Honda Element	$26,000			✓
One pair of jeans	$65		✓	
iPod	$249			✓
Cabin in the woods	$210,000			✓

Thirty days later, the list may look like **TABLE 5-5**:

TABLE 5-5

Sample Wish List, Round Three

Item Name	Cost	Need Today?	Need This Month?	Would Like Someday?
Smoothie maker	$30			✓
One pair of jeans	$65		✓	
iPod	$249			✓

At this point, you've narrowed your list to items you would clearly like to own and can begin to save for when your spending freeze is over. You also have a ready-made list if anyone asks you what you really want for your birthday.

Chapter 6

Saving Money on Groceries

This chapter helps you save money on some of your biggest expenses—food and incidentals. Whether you tend to eat out or in, whether or not you shop the sales, this chapter can help you find additional ways to cut a bit here and a bit there, adding up to real savings.

Preparing Your Own Meals

Even a generation or two ago, eating at restaurants used to be reserved for special occasions, and eating prepared foods was practically unheard of except among a few lifelong bachelors. Today, it's actually less common to make a meal from scratch than it is to eat at a restaurant, get take-out or fast food, or prepare a meal by mixing together ingredients from a box. Do people actually make meals from scratch?

Doing a Little Cooking

Yes, they do. One way to save hundreds of dollars every month is by making your own food. You don't even have to be very good at it: Even the least-seasoned chef can boil pasta and mix it with tomato sauce or broil a piece of chicken or beef. If you can make toast, you can cook. And the more you cook—even the easy stuff—the better you'll get at it; then you can progress to more difficult meals.

FACT

A great way to learn how to cook is to watch a cooking show and try to follow along in your own kitchen. If you watch a cooking show regularly (and in addition to Martha and Rachael, there are several cooking shows on cable and PBS), you can often go online to find a shopping list for the next episode.

The trick, of course, is that you have to take time out of your life to shop and cook, and most people don't have time these days. But if you're trying to meet your financial goals and don't have the opportunity to make more money, you can save a great deal of money by taking the time to cook. Keep in mind that because you pay income taxes, you can gain more ground by saving money than by earning more money.

Seeing How Much Eating Out Really Costs

To find out how much you can save, think about a plate of fettuccine Alfredo with chicken from a local restaurant. Visualize what's in a plateful, even if you don't know much about cooking. Offhand, you might guess that there's about a quarter pound of fettuccine, half a cup of cream, two tablespoons of butter, a quarter pound of chicken, and maybe a few other ingredients, but that's close enough. List the ingredients in your favorite dish on **WORKSHEET** 6-1, and the next time you're at the store, price it out. You can make a big portion of fettuccine Alfredo for about $2.90—it will cost at least $12.95, plus a tip, at your local Italian restaurant.

WORKSHEET 6-1
Grocery Versus Restaurant Comparison

Ingredient	Price to Buy at Store
	$
	$
	$
	$
	$
	$
	$
	$
	$
	$
	$
	$
TOTAL:	$

Of course, you won't get your meal prepared and served, but you also won't have to drive to the restaurant, wait in line, or pay a tip. Want to save money? Prepare your own food!

Not Letting Perishables Go Bad

If you tend to eat out a lot (or eat in with pizza, Chinese takeout, or other fast food), you may feel guilty about the fact that you're not cooking. To ease this guilt, you may go grocery shopping every week or two and buy vegetables, meats, dairy products, and other perishable foods, with the intention of changing your ways; but you don't change your ways, and the perishables go bad, and you throw them all out. A few weeks later, you start this vicious circle of wasted money all over again.

Here's the thing: Either decide you're going to have someone else cook for you, or decide you're going to cook for yourself. Neither way is inherently good or bad, but don't do both and waste food in the process. If you buy the food, stop eating out until it's gone. If you know you're going to eat out, don't buy the food. You could save a few hundred dollars a month.

Brown-Bagging It

If you go out to lunch every day—or even a few days a week—you can save quite a bit of money every month by bringing your lunch from home instead. It doesn't have to be fancy; in fact, if you make just a bit more than you need for dinner every night, you can pack the leftovers for lunch the next day. Or pack a sandwich, yogurt, and fruit—simple and cheap!

To find out how much you really spend on lunch, review your daily expense sheets in Chapter 2. Then make a sample menu for your lunches and write the ingredients in **WORKSHEET** **6-2,** comparing that total to your eating-out total.

If eating out at lunch is a big part of your social life, don't stop it completely. Instead, limit it to one day per week or a couple of days a month.

WORKSHEET 6-2
Brown-Bag Versus Eat-Out Lunch Comparison

Ingredient	Price to Buy at Store
	$
	$
	$
	$
	$
	$
	$
	$
	$
	$
	$
	$
	$
	$
TOTAL:	$

Using Coupons

Coupons are free money, but only if you use them for products you would have purchased anyway. Companies offer coupons because they want you to try their products, and they figure they'll give you a bonus for taking a risk, but this isn't how you save money on food. Instead, as you peruse coupons, cut out only the ones for products you already use or products that you're willing to use because you're not loyal to another brand. If, for example, you couldn't care less what kind of detergent you use, cut out all laundry coupons and use the ones that save you the most money. But if you never eat anything but Sugar Cereal for breakfast, don't cut out coupons for Fruity Cereal, no matter how much of a savings you'll get.

Even though cereal is considered a staple of the American diet, most cereal, with its refined flours and sugars, isn't really that good for you. And ounce for ounce, it's one of the most expensive foods in your grocery store. Eat more nutritionally dense food at breakfast, and you'll save money and still feel satisfied a few hours later.

Cutting out coupons is just the first step. To actually use them, you'll have to have them handy and organized. One cheap, simple way to keep them accessible is to put them in a 3" × 5" card–file box, organized by category. File the coupons under their appropriate categories, placing them in order by expiration date, so that the coupon that will expire first is the one you see first when you flip to that category. When you add new coupons, flip through each category to see whether you have any expired coupons that you need to toss out. Keep the box close to your keys so that you never forget to take it into the store with you. Or, if you tend to forget it, keep it in your car.

ESSENTIAL

Look for coupons in the Sunday paper, keeping in mind that coupons usually aren't offered the weekend of, or just before, a major holiday. Also, if you're buying the paper only for the coupons, make sure you're saving more than the cost of the paper each week.

Getting the Lowest Food Prices

The Sunday newspaper can be a great source of information about the cost of products in the stores in your area. Before you peruse the sale flyers, write out your weekly or monthly shopping list. Then look through that week's advertisements, noting on your shopping list which store has the best price on the items you need. Then make a quick stop at each store to buy only the items on sale that week.

Price Matching

If you have a store in your area that price matches—and most now do—you don't have to do all that running around. You simply inform the checkout clerk that you're going to price match an item, and you get the least expensive advertised price on that item.

E ALERT!

Don't forget to take the ads from other stores with you when you shop. Some stores absolutely will not honor price matches without checking the competitor's ad.

Buying Sale Items in Quantity

If you see a great sale price on an item that you use a lot—and if the item isn't perishable *and* you have the space to store it *and* you have enough money in this month's budget to pay for a large quantity *and* you're sure beyond a doubt that you will actually use this item up—buy a lot at the sale price. Suppose you make a tuna-fish sandwich for lunch every day and usually pay ninety-eight cents for each can of tuna. If you see it on sale for forty-nine cents, buy as much as you can store and afford, because you know you'll use it. But if you see bananas on sale, buy your usual amount. You can't possibly use up a large amount of bananas before they go bad.

Joining a Wholesale Club

One way to get sale prices every day is to shop at a wholesale club, such as Sam's Club or Costco. If you decide to go this route, make sure you're saving more money than the annual membership fee, and be sure that you don't spend more than you should in the name of "But it's such a good deal." Wholesale clubs can ruin your budget, so beware!

Some wholesale clubs offer memberships only to employees of small businesses, schools, churches, credit unions, and other groups. They also sometimes offer memberships to family members, friends, and neighbors of members. Others are open to the public. To join, call your local wholesale club to find out the membership requirements.

If you do buy at a wholesale club, apply the same logic that you would for buying large quantities of any sale item at your regular store: Buy bulk quantities only if you have the storage space, are sure you'll use it, can keep it from spoiling, and have the money in your budget to pay for it.

How much do wholesale clubs cost to join?
Most wholesale clubs cost from $35 to $50 to join, and you must renew your membership annually. Make sure you're saving more than this amount on your purchases, or the membership won't be worthwhile.

Growing a Garden, Even a Small One

If you eat a lot of veggies, you know they can be expensive. Yet for just a few dollars for the seeds, you can grow an entire garden of fresh vegetables every year. And if you have extras of easy-to-grow vegetables like tomatoes, you can freeze them for use in pasta sauces in the winter.

Using Your Patio or Balcony

Even if you don't have an extra acre out back to grow a garden, you can still raise vegetables. Many veggies grow well in outdoor containers on a patio or balcony, if you're careful to keep them well watered, well drained, and protected from freezing weather at night.

Growing Organically

To save money and protect your health, grow your vegetables organically. The trick to gardening without chemicals is to start with excellent soil. Improving your soil may cost you some money, but it'll pay off for years to come. To be sure, however, that you're actually getting more benefit from your garden than you're paying in soil, seeds or plants, and equipment, total up what you get out of your garden the first year and compare that to what you spent to get started.

If you're not going to be living in your house in three years, don't bother growing asparagus or planting fruit trees, which take several years to grow before they bear a harvest.

An alternative to growing your own garden is shopping at a farmer's market in your area. You'll usually pay lower prices than in a grocery store for fresher, less-processed fruits and vegetables. And you can still freeze the bounty when you find especially good deals on fresh produce.

Throwing a Budget-Friendly Party

Whether you're planning a birthday party, housewarming, graduation party, Fourth of July cookout, or even a wedding, don't let your party put you into debt. If you've budgeted for this party, stick to your budgeted amount like glue. If you haven't budgeted for it, determine from which areas you'll cut expenses so that you can free up some money without sacrificing your long-term financial goals.

Regardless of the type of event you're planning, you can do it tastefully while on a budget. The primary ways you can save money are as follows:

- **Host the event at home.** Host the event at your house or at the home of a good friend or relative, whether indoors or out. Renting a facility is one of the biggest budget-busters, because most rentals cost from a few hundred dollars to several thousand dollars. If your own home isn't appropriate and you can't borrow a home, consider other locations that might be free or low cost, such as the local beach or park.

- **Do your own decorations.** Browse stores like Hobby Lobby and Michaels for inexpensive centerpieces, candles, holiday greenery, and so on. And check out wholesale clubs for low-cost fresh flowers. Then gather your closest friends and have a preparty party, spending the day before or morning of your event doing a little decorating.

- **Pipe in your own music.** iPod players give you more options than ever. You can put together an entire evening's worth of music in a party playlist, and once you start the music, you won't have to think about it again the rest of the evening. If you don't have a sound system that plays an iPod, borrow one from a friend.

- **Cohost the event with others.** If, for example, your daughter's best friend is also graduating this year, consider hosting one party for the two of them, with both families sharing the expenses.

- **Keep it casual.** The fancier you make your event, the more your guests will expect, from tempting appetizers to expensive champagne. Think of it this way: If you're entertaining twenty-five people, a cookout will cost you far less than a formal dinner party will. And don't let tradition force a financial investment that will break your budget: A tasteful, well-planned cookout in a beautiful setting, where you serve delicious steaks and seafood, will be a dinner your guests will remember for years.

- **Keep it small.** Rather than throwing a party for forty people every year, consider inviting four friends or colleagues to dinner, and then repeating that every month or two with different friends. You'll spread out your expenses and, in the long run, probably spend less because you won't have to decorate, purchase appetizers, send invitations, and so on.

- **Cater it yourself.** By shopping at wholesale clubs or restaurant-supply stores, you can buy large quantities of prepared foods that are practically guaranteed to taste great. The trick is two-fold: 1) Read all cooking instructions well in advance of the party so that you know when to start dishes so they're all ready at the same time; and 2) make sure you have enough oven space to cook all the items at the same time. If not, see whether you can borrow your neighbors' ovens in advance of the party.

- **Keep appetizers simple.** You don't have to serve shrimp and caviar. Combine fresh vegetables, pita-bread pieces, and hummus for one appetizer; serve blue corn chips and salsa for another; and prepare fruit chunks on skewers as a third. All are festive, tasty, and far less expensive appetizers than the more formal budget-busters.
- **Send e-vites.** Don't spend money on stamps; instead, send free e-vites via e-mail. Evite (*www.evite.com*) is the biggest electronic invitation company. The Web site also offers party-planning ideas.

QUESTION?

How much do electronic invitations cost to send?
From Evite (and most other companies), electronic invitations are free. You choose an invitation design, enter information about your shindig, and send the invitation to your e-mail list. Guests then accept or decline. You can also send a reminder or updates (such as weather-related venue changes) just before the event.

- **Make it a potluck meal, and you provide desserts, appetizers, and beverages.** You can throw an elegant party by asking guests to bring a main dish, and you provide an array of delicious appetizers, gourmet desserts, and beverages. You won't have to cook and will save on the most expensive part of the meal.
- **Make it a cooking or baking party.** Whether you're throwing a child's birthday party or an engagement party for your best friend, to cut down on costs, include a cooking or baking component, with each guest bringing one key ingredient. Whether you're baking cookies, making fondue, or having a chili cook-off, you'll not only create an interesting party theme, you'll cut down substantially on your expenses.

Chapter 7

Cutting Your Expenses at Home

If you're having trouble putting together a balanced budget, take a look at this chapter, which gives you eleven solid ideas for cutting your expenses at home right now. Each one by itself may not save you tons of money, but if you combine several of them, over time the savings will add up.

Turning the Thermostat Down (or Up)

A simple way to cut your heating and cooling costs is to turn your thermostat down one degree in winter and up one degree in summer. One degree— which you probably won't even notice—can save you up to a hundred dollars a year on your heating and cooling bills.

FACT

Programmable thermostats are available at all home-improvement stores and cost between $35 and $75, depending on the features they offer. Look for one that has both weekday and weekend settings, especially if you tend to wake up later in the morning on Saturdays and Sundays.

Using a programmable thermostat is a simple way to do this. These thermostats automatically turn your temperatures up and down at preset times. So if you are always in bed by 11:00 in the winter, you program the thermostat to turn down the heat at 11:15, saving you money all night. It then turns the temperature back up at 6:30 in the morning, so you wake up to a toasty house. It turns the temperature down again while you're away at work and turns it up just before you get home. These thermostats are easy to program—look for one that offers daytime and nighttime settings, plus separate settings for the weekend, when you're likely to be home more and sleep in later. Because programmable thermostats actually turn the temperature down, they pay for themselves in a couple of months.

Getting Your Books and DVDs from the Library

One of the best-kept secrets in budgeting circles is that your local library lets you borrow stuff for free. From books to CDs, DVDs, and audio books, your library has a wide range of free opportunities to entertain you and your family. And library cards are also free.

ALERT!

Whatever you do, don't return your books and DVDs late! The point here is to save money, not spend it. Although fines on books are often just twenty-five cents per day, that's per book, so if you have more than one, you'll pay more. And fines on DVDs and CDs can run $1–$2 per day, each. If you're not careful, you can end up owing the library $23—wait, that's my story, not yours!

Getting Rid of Cable/Satellite and/or Your Phone Land Line

Although you may think that cable or satellite TV is part of life's necessities, they're really just extra services that you should subscribe to only if you have plenty of extra money each month—after you pay all of your other financial obligations. It is possible to live without them, and you'll read a whole lot more if you get rid of your TV altogether.

If you're using your cell phone most of the time anyway, consider getting rid of your land line, too.

Because you're probably cutting way back on your expenses, don't overlook these simple ways to save a lot of money. Prices for these services vary greatly from one area to another, but here's an example:

- **Cable:** $43 per month × 12 months = $396 per year
- **Land line:** $47 per month × 12 months = $348 per year
- **Total Annual Savings:** $1,080 per year

Think of this: If you're currently trying to pay off $2,500 in credit card debt and make no other changes to your income or expenses except to get rid of your cable service and land line, you'll be debt-free in less than two-and-a-half years. And you'll save even more if you are paying for premium movie channels or if your land line has several premium features or offers free long distance.

Okay, so perhaps you accept the idea that these services do cost money and that you'd be in better financial shape if you got rid of them. Your sense of resistance comes from not knowing how you could possibly live without them. The following sections share some tips.

Alternatives to Cable and Satellite

Instead of subscribing to cable or satellite TV, which offers you dozens or even hundreds of channels to choose from, record every network and public-television program you think you'd enjoy onto an eight- or twelve-hour video cassette. Also, as friends switch from VCR to DVD, ask whether you can have their old videos. Build up a collection of favorites to rewatch anytime the urge strikes. Don't forget your public library, either: most loan DVDs of movies, documentaries, and miniseries free of charge, and some even loan popular series, too.

ALERT!

If you're using cable, satellite, or DSL to connect to the Internet, be sure to find an alternative before getting rid of these services. To connect via cable or satellite, you need to be subscribing to those services in some way. To connect via DSL, you must have a land line.

If you get such terrible reception in your area that you can't even watch TV without cable or satellite, you have two low-cost choices. One is to sign up for just the basic cable coverage, which gives you network stations, public television, and perhaps a few other stations, a feature that usually costs $10 to $15 per month. The other is to stop watching TV broadcasts and either only watch DVDs or stop watching TV altogether. Keep in mind that many TV shows are now available on DVD approximately four or five months after the last season episode airs.

One final alternative is to subscribe to Netflix (*www.netflix.com*) or a similar DVD rental program, through which you receive between one and three DVD rentals at a time (movies, documentaries, and TV shows), sent to your home. Returns are free, and as soon as you return a DVD, another is sent to you right away, based on a list you create of hundreds or thousands of DVDs you want to rent, in order of priority. Plans run from about $6 per month to $20 per month. Movies are even downloadable via the Internet.

Alternatives to a Land Line

The obvious alternative to a land line is a cell [...]
rid of your land line will increase your need for [...]
pay a higher fee for that), double check your ma [...]
companies are offering their customers: Free in [...]
weekends; night-time rates starting earlier than [...]
ers on the same network; free text messagin [...]
tract is up, if you can switch to another cell co [...]
not having a land line, go for it!

Shopping Around for Car Insurance and Reducing Your Deductibles

Consider the following story: A Midwestern couple who lives in a small town pays nearly $1,150 per year for insurance on their two cars. They don't drive far to work, haven't had any accidents or received any speeding tickets, and they own their own home, so they're a good risk. They think $1,150 per year isn't too much to spend—it's on par with what their neighbors pay, and it's less than they paid when they lived in a larger city. They have an agent, but they haven't seen or spoken to her in years, and if they do have an accident, they are supposed to call a toll-free number, not the agent.

Then they see an ad for Progressive Insurance. They call the number to get its price and the price of three competing insurance companies. (Here's where the story gets a little unbelievable.) For the exact same coverage, Progressive offers them insurance for $385 per year, a savings of $765 per year! You're thinking this is a made-up story, right? Nope—all true. This scenario happened about five years go, and the service and coverage has been exactly the same—maybe even better because Progressive has a twenty-four-hour customer-service hotline that's operated seven days a week. The moral of the story is this: Shop around. Insurance companies change their products and prices all the time. Once a year, do a quick Internet search of insurance prices, and if you find a substantially lower price, ask your current agent to requote your policy to see whether he or she can match what you've found.

Keep in mind that speeding, reckless driving, and driving under the influence can ruin your finances. Not only will you get socked with the soaring cost of tickets, but your insurance rates could double or triple.

Comparison Shopping

You have nothing to lose—and potentially a lot of money to gain—by contacting Progressive at 800-PROGRESSIVE or *www.progressive.com*. Keep in mind that if you've received a lot of traffic tickets, have been in one or more accidents, live in an area that tends to produce a lot of accidents or car thefts, drive a car that's expensive to repair, or have a very long commute, your insurance payment may be quite a bit higher than the example given here. But because Progressive gives you the insurance rate for its major competitors, you may find a non-Progressive rate that's still better than what you're paying now. Use **WORKSHEET 7-1** as a handy place to compare rates and coverage.

WORKSHEET 7-1
Insurance Comparisons

Insurance Company	Semiannual Premium	Type of Coverage
	$	
	$	
	$	
	$	
	$	
	$	
	$	
	$	
	$	
	$	
	$	

Raising Your Deductibles

If your insurance payments are still uncomfortably high after you shop around, try raising your deductibles (the amount you pay out of pocket if you have an accident, your car is stolen, or a flood washes your car away). You can save quite a bit on your annual insurance costs by increasing your deductibles from $250 to $500 or from $500 to $1,000 (per incident). Some companies don't offer high deductibles, but if yours does, see how much of a difference raising it can make. Do be sure, though, to put the amount of your deductible in a savings account so the money is there if you need to repair your car.

Avoiding Extended Warranties

No matter what major purchase you make—car, furnace, computer, or dishwasher—you'll probably be offered an extended warranty by the company selling you the product. For "just" $79, you can add an extra year to the existing warranty. Sometimes you can even add three or four years of protection. These extended warranties can be a good investment in some cases, but they're a bad idea at other times.

When Not to Buy an Extended Warranty

If the product you're purchasing has any of the following characteristics, steer clear of an extended warranty:

- You intend to own the product for only as long as the original warranty is in effect.
- Within a few years, the product will be out of date, and you'll want or need to get a better, more powerful model.
- The purchase price is low enough that you wouldn't be strapped if you had to buy another in a few years.
- Repairing this product is simple and inexpensive.
- The cost of this product is likely to decrease over the next few years.
- The extended warranty costs more than 20 percent of the purchase price.

When to Buy an Extended Warranty

Do get an extended warranty if any of the following is true for you:

- This piece of equipment is critical to your livelihood.
- You know you can't afford to replace the product if it breaks.
- The warranty is a very good deal.

ALERT!

Check out the insurance company before you buy an extended warranty. Look into how long it has been in business (call the company's 800 number or check its Web site) and call the Better Business Bureau (BBB) in your area to find out whether this company will even be in business in three years.

You can set up your own "extended warranty" savings account. If the product you're buying costs $120 and comes with a one-year warranty, put $10 per month into your savings account. When the year is up, you'll have enough money in savings to cover the purchase of a new product, should the old one break. If the cost of the product tends to go up with time, as is the case with a car, put a little more than the existing cost into your savings account.

Buying Reliable, High-Quality Products

This idea may seem to go against most money-saving advice, but the truth is that high-quality products tend to last longer. If you buy a well-researched, reliable car instead of an inexpensive economy car, you'll pay substantially more. But if the economy car fizzles in three years and the Volvo keeps running for fifteen years after that, you'll probably save money in the long run.

Keep the following tips in mind, however, when shopping for quality:

- If buying the quality item will wreck your budget, either save up and come back when you can afford it or make do with the less expensive item.
- Don't automatically assume that higher price equals higher quality. Sometimes higher prices are simply the result of savvy businesspeople thinking that consumers will associate their products with quality if they charge a lot.
- If you aren't sure how to recognize reliability and quality, check out *Consumer Reports,* your best source for honest, detailed testing results for tens of thousands of products. If *Consumer Reports* thinks a product has problems with quality, keep shopping. Because they don't accept advertising dollars, their testing results are unbiased. Most libraries have subscriptions to this publication, so if you're willing to do a bit of research, you can get the information for free.
- Don't worry about buying a quality product if you're not planning to keep it very long. If you're on vacation and forget your swimsuit, don't spend a lot for another one—just buy something that will see you through.

Not Buying Trendy Items

Before you buy anything, ask yourself whether you're buying it because it's the best-quality item you can get for the price or because it's a hip, happening item that makes you feel good for the moment. Women's shoes and purses come to mind as short-term, trendy items that tend to be out of style in a year or two.

Many budgets are blown on novelty items, and what's so frustrating about buying them is that a couple of weeks or months later, you can't figure out what you saw in the item in the first place! Before you buy anything, apply the one-year test: Is this an item you'll want a year from now? If not, pass it up.

Becoming a Late Adopter

You don't have to be the first kid on your block to get everything. Personal electronics, especially, tend to have a high initial price, and then settle into a lower price for late adopters. For example, iPods of all shapes and sizes are now available at Sam's Club for less than you'd pay elsewhere, but it takes a while for the latest colors and models to reach the discount stores. Give it a few months, and then make your purchase—if you budgeted for the item!

Shopping Tag Sales, Resale Shops, and Online Auctions

Whether you're furnishing a nursery or building a wardrobe, tag sales (also called garage sales or yard sales) and resale shops, including those from Goodwill Industries and The Salvation Army, can save you a bundle.

Does this go against the advice in the preceding section to buy high-quality items? Not necessarily. Just because an item is being sold at a tag sale or resale shop doesn't mean it isn't a high-quality item. The mere fact that the item has lasted long enough to be worn by someone until it no longer fit or went out of fashion or the person became bored with it points to the fact that this is a long-lasting product. Cheaply made products don't usually end up at tag sales and resale shops—instead, they get thrown out.

Some low-quality items do appear, however, so you need to know a couple of tricks for shopping at tag sales and resale shops. These techniques are discussed in the following sections.

Preparing a Shopping List Ahead of Time

If you just go to browse, you're likely to end up buying something that you don't need; even the deepest discount isn't a bargain if you don't need the item. Before you leave home, determine your needs and put them down on paper—and then don't buy anything that's not on your list, no matter how wonderful or how cheap it is.

Purchasing High-Quality, Undamaged Products

If you're interested in an item, pick it up and carry it with you. If you're not sure you want it and don't pick it up, it's liable to be gone when you go back to look for it, especially at a tag sale. At large resale shops like Goodwill Industries and The Salvation Army, you may never again find that blue shirt among the hundreds of blue shirts they stock.

After you've looked at everything you're interested in, turn to the items you've been carrying. Look closely at any product before buying it. Examine it for damage of any sort; turn it over and inside out to see whether it's cheaply made or is something that will last a while. Keep in mind that even buying a $2 chair or a $1 pair of pants isn't a good deal if it breaks or rips the first time you use it.

Consider Haggling—or Not

A lot of people haggle at garage sales. Most people holding the sales expect it, but the choice is up to you. You may save a few bucks, but the person having the garage sale is also trying to make some money, so if the marked price seems acceptable to you, pay it.

Winning at Auctions

If there's an item you've been looking for but can't quite afford, get yourself over to an online auction site (such as eBay, at *www.eBay.com*) to see whether anyone is offering it at less-than-retail value. You can search for items by keywords (better than browsing, which is too tempting), and you may be given two options: An option to submit a bid, and an option to buy it immediately at a set price. If that buy-it-now price is lower than what you'd pay elsewhere, be sure to check what the shipping and handling charges will be.

If you decide to bid on an item, be sure to utilize the automatic bidding function, that will keep electronically raising your bid until you reach your highest price. This will keep you from having to be notified each time someone outbids you; it also forces you to set your highest price well in advance, so that you don't get caught up in a bidding euphoria and blow your budget. If you're afraid you'll be tempted to bid higher than the limit you originally set, be sure to be away from e-mail in the final minutes before the auction expires.

Reducing Gift Expenditures

Contrary to popular belief, you don't have to purchase gifts for your friends, family, and coworkers on every birthday, anniversary, or Hallmark holiday. You can, for example, save money on holiday gifts by drawing names among your friends, family, and/or coworkers. For any occasion, you can give a small donation to a favorite charity in the name of the gift recipient and send a card explaining the gift. Consider making gifts as well: Cookies, breads, soups, and so on. Also, anyone—from a close friend, to a casual acquaintance, to a family member you don't see often—will appreciate a simple, handwritten note from you.

One way to save on gifts is not to give them at all! Let friends, family, and coworkers know that while you're getting your finances under control, you won't be giving—and don't expect to get—presents for the next few years. Send a note to this effect in late September or early October to give people time to adjust!

Avoiding Dry-Cleaning

Unless the product you're cleaning absolutely, positively has to be dry-cleaned (check the label), don't use this expensive service. Many articles of clothing—even silk, wool, and linen—can be hand washed or washed using the delicate cycle of your washer, using an extra-mild detergent.

QUESTION?

What if I must dry-clean an item I own?
If you do need to dry-clean a product, be sure to check your Sunday paper or local coupon book for reduced rates. You may be able to get from 10 to 30 percent off.

Taking Cheaper Vacations

Advertising on TV and in magazines may lead you to believe that the only way you can be a good spouse or parent is to take your family on a cruise, to Disney World, or to sunny vacation spots in the winter. Remember the source, though: These advertisements come from places that need you to visit in order for them to make money!

ALERT!

If you plan to take a vacation this year, be sure to estimate the taxes on hotel rooms, rental cars, and meals. In some areas, these taxes can total nearly 20 percent!

The truth is, though, that for a vacation to be great, all you need to do is get out of your current environment for a while, doing something fun and, perhaps, different. To save money on your vacation, for example, you can stay right in your own state, perhaps in an area you've never visited before. Plan to stay in an extended-stay hotel, which will usually have a kitchenette so you can cook your own meals and which offers discounts for stays of seven nights or more. If you already own camping equipment, consider going that route. Pack picnic lunches and look for free or low-cost attractions, such as museums, parks, zoos, and so on. Hiking is nearly always free and is a great way to find new adventures.

ESSENTIAL

To save money on certain hotel rooms, get a copy of the discount coupon guides for the area you'll be visiting by going to *www.roomsaver .com* or *www.hotelcoupons.com*. These guides are also often available at rest stops and fast-food restaurants in the area. The coupons in these travel guides save you from 15 to 50 percent on room costs—making them even lower than standard Internet rates. You can also find other hotel deals by searching the Net for "discount hotels" and the name of the geographic area you'll be visiting.

Remember that just because you're on vacation, you don't have a license to spend money that you would never dream of spending at home. To keep shopping extravaganzas to a limit, consider bringing traveler's checks or a check card (a debit card, but with a cap) for all your vacation expenses, including hotel, rental cars, and so on. Instead of putting your vacation on a credit card, use your traveler's checks or check card, which some banks offer free or at a reduced rate. You'll get nervous as you see them dwindle and won't be tempted to buy souvenirs or other unplanned items.

Chapter 8

Reducing Your Biggest Expenses

If your financial obligations exceed your income by so much that creating a budget seems impossible right now, take steps to cut your biggest expenses over the next few months and years. These are not easy cuts to make, but they can help you get back on solid financial footing.

Moving to a Smaller House

Real-estate agents and mortgage lenders can be awfully generous with your money. When you go house hunting, both will tell you that you can afford a lot of house—it's in their best interest to do so. Real-estate agents are paid a percentage of the price of the house you buy, and mortgage lenders earn their money on fees and interest that rise with the purchase price of your home.

But neither of these parties has any interest in helping you manage your money over the long haul. Even mortgage lenders only care about whether you'll repay the loan on time, not whether you can barely make ends meet or are getting yourself deeper into credit card debt each year.

Real-estate agents and mortgage lenders aren't the only people who influence you to want to live in a big, expensive house. Advertising, movies, TV shows, and other forms of media send a clear message that the bigger and more expensive your house, the more you should be respected in this world.

Worried that you won't be able to fit all your stuff into a smaller house? Just accept that you won't fit it all in, hold a tag sale (see Chapter 9), and get rid of as much of it as you can! Everyone buys enough stuff to fill whatever size house they're currently living in.

Thinking "Not So Big"

Want to get on solid financial footing? Then forget what society and your friends, family, and coworkers say about big houses. Instead, put your house up for sale and set out to find the smallest house in the best neighborhood with the best schools. House prices are usually based on square footage, quality, and location—location often being the most important. (This is why tiny, fixer-upper, ocean-view houses can cost ten or twenty times more than similar houses inland.) You don't want to skimp on quality and location; instead, the trick is to reduce your square footage.

You can probably live in half the square footage you're living in now if you pare down some of your belongings and live more efficiently. (At your local library, flip through a copy of *The Not So Big House* by Sarah Susanka [Taunton Press, 2001], along with several spin-off books in the same vein.) So aim for this: If you're living in a 2,500-square-foot house, look at houses that are 1,200 or 1,300 square feet. If you find this is just too cramped for your family, move up 100 to 300 square feet, but not much more than that. Your new house has to be substantially cheaper to make the move worthwhile (see **WORKSHEET 8-1**).

Considering the Costs of Moving

You will have expenses associated with moving, but if you move to a house that saves you enough money each month, those expenses will be worthwhile. (If you need to, you can even finance the costs of getting a new mortgage right into your monthly payments. And if credit card debt is crushing you, you may also be able to pay off those credit cards at the same time—see Chapters 9 and 10 for details.) **WORKSHEET 8-1** helps you work through some of the costs of staying versus moving.

WORKSHEET 8-1

Moving Versus Staying

Expense	If You Move	If You Stay
Monthly mortgage	$	$
Closing costs	$	$0
Utilities	$	$
Moving costs	$	$0
Expected repairs	$	$

Keep in mind that if you're in a poor financial situation, mortgage lenders may not approve you for a loan right now. Before you put your current house up for sale, get preapproved for a mortgage. You don't want to sell your house and then find that you aren't in a position to get another mortgage at this time.

ALERT!

Try to finance your new mortgage for the exact same number of years (or very close) that you have left on your current mortgage. Sure, your monthly payments will be lower if you increase the life of your loan, but you'll weaken your financial future in the process.

Buying a House Instead of Renting

If you're currently paying a hefty monthly rent on your house or apartment, consider buying a house. Keep in mind that buying a house isn't always a good idea—in fact, when you're strapped for money and/or in debt, it may be a terrible idea. You may have trouble qualifying for a mortgage, and you might end up paying more (in the short term) for a house in property taxes, homeowner's insurance, maintenance, and repairs. (See Chapter 17 for further details.)

Assuming you can qualify for a mortgage (and it's always a good idea to get preapproved by a lender—a process that's usually free), consider the following two situations that make financial sense when you're thinking of buying a house:

- You can mortgage a house that has some repair and maintenance needs on a fifteen-year loan for 60 percent (or less) of what you pay now.
- You can mortgage a new, quality house for fifteen years for the same or a little more than you're paying now.

In the first situation, you'll see an immediate improvement in your financial situation, but down the road, you may incur maintenance and repair costs that can add up. In the second situation, you won't see much of a change in your immediate financial picture, but you'll reap major benefits in the future.

Why the emphasis on fifteen-year loans? Because so much more of your payment goes toward principal (instead of interest) with a fifteen-year loan, so you can build a substantial amount of equity in your home in just five years. With a fifteen-year loan, you'll pay off over 23 percent of your debt in the first five years. With a thirty-year loan, you'll pay off just under 6 percent in those same five years.

WORKSHEET 8-2 helps you decide whether buying is better than renting for your specific situation.

WORKSHEET 8-2
Buying Versus Renting

Rent		Buy	
Monthly payment*	$	Monthly payment	$
Renter's insurance	$	Homeowner's insurance	$
Utilities	$	Utilities	$
		Property taxes	$
		Maintenance (estimate)	$
		Homeowner's-association dues	$
Total per month	$	Total per month	$
× 360**		× 360**	
Thirty-Year Cost	$	Thirty-Year Cost	$

Keep in mind that your rent is likely to rise sharply over the next thirty years!

**If you plan to mortgage your house for fifteen years, multiply by 180.*

Note: *This worksheet does not take into account the potential tax savings associated with home ownership.*

QUESTION?

Why do experts think having a mortgage is a good type of debt?
Because the price of houses tends to appreciate (go up) with time, so when people sell their homes, they can pay off the debt on the house and still have plenty of money left over. In addition, you get a rare tax break on the interest you pay on your mortgage.

Renting Instead of Buying

Wait—doesn't this section say just the opposite of everything the last section touted? It does, but owning a house isn't for everyone—nor is it always the most economical way to go. If you're planning to live in an area for two years or less, if you live in an area that has very high real-estate costs, or if interest rates are quite high, stick to renting for a while.

Rethinking Your Ideas about Transportation

Cars can cost a lot of money: Payments or leases usually run several hundred dollars a month; maintenance and repairs are expensive; over-the-top gasoline prices can squeeze your budget; and registration and insurance can set you back a thousand dollars or more each year.

Looking into Public Transportation

If you live in an area where you can walk or bike to work and the grocery store, or if you have a reliable mass-transit system in your area, consider getting rid of your car.

Many people wonder how you'll get home for the holidays or take vacations if you don't have a car. The simplest solution is to rent a car when you need one. You may pay a lot for the rental five or six times a year, but that cost won't come close to the amount you now pay in car payments, insurance, maintenance, and so on.

To most people this is a revolutionary—if not repulsive—idea. Having a car is like having a name: Everybody has one! Well, actually, they don't. Plenty of people who live in large cities don't own cars, and they love it. And more and more environmentalists are touting the benefits of walking or biking or riding public transportation to work, so you're not completely alone there, either.

Even if you're not a city dweller or staunch friend of the earth, getting rid of your car can make sense. There's an immediate financial impact. If you're making monthly car payments, those will stop right away. And if your car is paid off, you'll get some cash that will help you pay your other bills.

Going the Bicycle or Vespa Route

Even if public transportation in your area isn't up to par, you may still be able to live without a car, especially if you live in an area with a mild climate. Cycling to work every day gives you two immediate benefits: 1) It saves you money; and 2) it gets you into shape. Many companies now offer a shower at work, so if you get sweaty on the ride in, you can shower and change into work clothes when you get there. By installing a pack on your bike (called townies) that holds two sacks of groceries, you can also stop by the store on your way home.

If being completely reliant on your physical prowess to get you around town is a little much for you, consider investing in a moped, such as the popular Vespas. These economical vehicles are like low-powered motorcycles, and generally run from $800 (used) to about $2,000 (gleaming and new). If you can sell your car, buy a Vespa, and saving bundles in gas, insurance, and registration might make getting a little wind-blown not seem so bad.

Keeping a Paid-Off, Reliable Car

Note that if you have a reliable car that's paid off, runs well, and costs a reasonable amount in gasoline, maintenance, and insurance, you're probably better off not selling it. A car like this is just too rare to part with.

Another situation in which selling your car isn't a good idea is if you're upside down in your loan—that means your car is worth less than you owe on it. If you're upside down in your loan and interest rates are lower than they were when you bought the car, look into refinancing your car loan.

Next time you buy a car, purchase the highest-quality model you can afford, put as much money down on it as you can, and arrange for the fewest number of payments possible. Then plan to drive the car—payment-free—for as many years as you can after you pay it off.

Deciding Between a Hummer and a MINI

If you're in the market for a car (new or used), you'll need to make an important decision: Hummer or MINI. Another way to put this is, are you going to go with a roomy interior and low mpg, or a small interior and high mpg? The MINI (and similar small or hybrid cars) offers a few advantages:

- **They cost less.** Sure, you can get a souped-up MINI (the S version, in the convertible, with all the available packages and options), but even that's not going to cost you as much as a Hummer. If you finance your car, this means that your monthly payments will be lower or you'll be able to finance your car for fewer months.
- **They get much better mileage.** This has substantial financial ramifications over the next several years, especially given the recent jack in gas prices.
- **Your auto insurance may be cheaper.** This didn't used to be the case, as smaller cars were also often less safe, so insurance for smaller cars wasn't any less than for larger ones. But today's small cars often do just as well in crash tests as larger, more expensive cars, and because the smaller cars cost less to replace, insurance companies charge less in premiums.
- **You can park in all those parking-garage spaces that say "Compact cars only."** Finding parking for a smaller car is always easier.

Choosing Between Leasing and Buying

Except for a few business-related tax breaks, leasing a car will never improve your financial picture. Leasing a car amounts to borrowing it for a specified number of months or years and, at the end of your contract, giving it back. Leasing is attractive to many people because your monthly payments are lower than when you buy and the length of a lease contract is usually fairly short, which means you can get a new car more often than if you buy. But leasing it is really just having a long-term rental car.

If you must own a car, don't lease! Instead, buy a reliable car on the fewest number of payments you can afford and plan to drive it for ten years. After you've paid it off, keep making the payments to your savings account so that you can pay cash for your next car.

In order to improve your financial picture, stop thinking of a car as an extension of who you are. Ultimately, if you're miserable because you're sinking deeper and deeper into debt and/or don't know how you're going to pay your bills this month, who cares what you're driving? You also want to stop thinking of a car payment as a fact of life. Just imagine how much more breathing room you'd have each month if you didn't have a car payment. Well, leasing never lets you go there. You're locked in to making a payment every month, and when you're done paying, you still don't own a car. You just have to go out and get another one, and make the lease payments on it for several more years.

Changing Jobs

Getting a different job can have a variety of immediate impacts, each discussed in the following sections.

A New Job Can Increase Your Paycheck

A job is always more than just a paycheck. Depending on the job you have, it can be an opportunity to test yourself, develop new skills, meet all sorts of new people, travel, express yourself, see your values turned into action, and so on.

If you're looking for a short-term boost in income, look into part-time freelancing opportunities (work you complete at home, evenings and weekends) or whether you can work overtime (see Chapter 11). Keep in mind, too, that most afternoon and evening shifts pay a premium to compensate you for the odd hours you'll be working.

When your financial situation is bleak, however, the paycheck can be the most important aspect of having a job. Whatever you do, don't take a job with no growth or one that is in direct opposition to your values just for the money—unless you can guarantee that the job is temporary. If you think you can make more money at another job, however, do begin your search immediately. Even if you end up turning down another job offer, knowing what other jobs pay—and what other companies expect from you—is well worth the time spent searching.

Don't forget to look within your own company for a higher-paying job. Let your supervisor know that you're itching for more responsibility, and keep your eye on internal job postings. Take advantage of any training the company offers. In addition, find out what skills and training the job you have in mind calls for and see whether your company will pay for (or reimburse you for) classes at your local college or job-training site.

A New Job Can Reduce Your Commute

Reducing or eliminating your commute (which can happen if you find a job that lets you telecommute) means that you save gas and maintenance on your car. You may also, potentially, eliminate the need for a car altogether. Although many people commute more than an hour each way, commuting isn't free and it can take a toll on your finances—see **WORKSHEET 8-3.**

WORKSHEET 8-3
Costs of Commuting

Tangible Costs	Amount You Pay
Gasoline	$
Oil changes	$
Tune-ups	$
	$
	$

Intangible Costs	What You Give Up
Wasted time	
Frustration	
TOTAL:	$

A New Job Can Reduce or Eliminate Your Insurance Costs

If you pay more for your medical, dental, and life insurance than you can afford, look for a job that offers these benefits free or subsidizes them. Even if the job pays a lower salary, your bottom line may improve by having these benefits paid for. Use **WORKSHEET 8-4** to help you decide.

Note that you'll first need to figure out the amount you pay every two weeks for insurance. If you pay for it on your own every month, divide that by 2.165. If you pay it semiannually, divide by 13; if you pay annually, divide by 26. If your employer takes it out of your paycheck every two weeks, use the amount shown on your pay stub.

You'll also need to know your gross income every two weeks on your current job and on the job you're considering. Gross income is the amount you're paid before taxes and deductions are taken out of your check. This is often stated as an hourly wage (say, $9.50 per hour) or as an annual salary ($19,000 per year). To find this amount, look on your pay stub for the amount listed as "gross income."

WORKSHEET 8-4
Benefits Analysis

Current job: Gross income per paycheck	
Insurance benefit deducted per paycheck or	
Insurance paid monthly	–
Current job: Income minus insurance costs	**$**
New job: Gross income per paycheck	
Insurance benefit deducted per paycheck (if any)	–
New job: Income minus insurance costs	**$**

Whichever income line is higher is your better bet for the time being.

A New Job Can Reduce or Eliminate What You Pay for Child Care

Some companies offer free or subsidized day care, either in the company's facility or at a day-care center close by. If child-care costs are putting your finances in jeopardy, seek out a company that offers this benefit (also see Chapter 16 for more on calculating the costs of day care).

If your child-care costs are high, consider getting a job with a company that offers day care, even if the job pays a lower salary. But be sure that the company offers a good insurance plan for your family. Use **WORKSHEET 8-5** to help you, keeping in mind that gross income is the amount you make before taxes and deductions are taken out and that, for this worksheet, your paycheck is assumed to arrive every two weeks.

Working Mother magazine's annual listing of the best companies to work for includes child-care assistance as a criterion. As you're searching for a new job, use this list to find companies that offer the atypical benefit of on-site day care.

WORKSHEET 8-5
Child Care Analysis

Current job: Gross income per paycheck	
Insurance benefit deducted per paycheck	–
Weekly day-care costs multiplied by 2	–
Current job: Income minus insurance and day-care costs	**$**
New job: Gross income per paycheck	
Insurance benefit deducted per paycheck (if any)	–
Day-care benefit deducted per paycheck (if any)	–
New job: Income minus insurance and day-care costs	**$**

A New Job Can Reduce Your Need for an Expensive Wardrobe

Although this may seem like a silly benefit to consider when changing jobs, the costs of buying and caring for clothing can add up throughout the year. If you're able to find a job that allows you to dress casually, with clothes you already own and can wash in a washing machine, you can save a bundle. **TABLE 8-6** gives an example:

TABLE 8-6
Sample Clothing Savings

Existing Job (Annual Expenses)	New Job (Annual Expenses)
Suits, ties, shoes: $650	Khakis, knit shirts, loafers: $300
Dry cleaning: $525	Machine washing: $150
TOTAL: $1,175	TOTAL: $450

For this example, your annual savings amounts to $725. That's enough to buy a DVD player and about fifty DVDs! Or almost enough for a computer or a new sofa or new casual clothes for two more years.

Chapter 9

Restructuring a Heavy Debt Burden

If your debts are crushing you, you may need to take action to restructure them through a number of means: Credit counseling; debt consolidation; or selling some of your assets. This chapter helps you understand the basics of debt restructuring.

9

Understanding How Debt Is Restructured

Does this sound like you? You have too much debt to handle—maybe you've charged more than you can afford on several credit cards, you have school loans plus a car and house payment, and the usual payments for utilities and food. You're having trouble making monthly payments, perhaps you are already a few months behind, and you're starting to be (or have been for some time) hassled by debt collectors. If so, debt restructuring is exactly what you need! The idea is that you change the way your debt is structured by lowering interest rates, lengthening repayment schedules, combining several payments into one smaller payment, or getting some of the debts forgiven, and at the same time, you stop getting further into debt. You may have to give something up, but you'll probably come out way ahead in the long run.

ALERT!

If you've been using a check-cashing service to get cash for your paycheck (or a cash loan against your next paycheck), stop immediately! Most of these companies charge a ridiculous amount of money for their services. Instead, open a bank account (look for a totally free one), which you can open with anywhere from $5 to $50.

There are a number of ways to restructure your current debts. You might see a credit counselor to discuss your options (this is often a good place to begin because it's usually free), consolidate most of your debts into one payment, sell some of your assets, use the equity in your house to pay off your debts (see Chapter 10), or declare bankruptcy (see Chapter 14). This chapter gives you the details of each option.

Getting Credit Counseling

Credit counseling is usually a free, nonprofit service that offers an alternative to bankruptcy. Each agency assigns you a counselor who reviews your debts, assets, income, and so on, to help you identify your options other than bankruptcy. Sometimes the credit counselors are bona fide financial gurus, but more often they're simply well-trained, well-meaning volunteers who offer an excellent service. All credit-counseling agencies offer their services in complete confidentiality and may offer services over the phone and Internet, as well as in face-to-face consultations.

Keep in mind, however, that not all credit-counseling agencies are nonprofit, and some are almost like scams. You can find out more in the "Consolidating Your Debt" section in this chapter.

Making Sure the Counseling Is Free

Your initial counseling session(s) should be completely free. If it isn't, get out as fast as you can! Many wonderful nonprofit credit-counseling agencies exist, so don't waste your money on an agency that charges you for counseling. While you may have to pay a small fee to consolidate your debt, the counseling session itself—in which your finances are sorted out and advice is offered—should be free.

Getting Comfortable with Your Counselor

Be sure you trust your counselor and feel confident in his or her abilities. If you don't, find out whether you can have another counselor assigned to you. Keep in mind, however, that your agency is probably a nonprofit organization with limited resources. You should have a darned good reason for wanting to be assigned a new counselor before you ask for this special treatment.

Taking Advantage of Free Financial-Education Opportunities

Credit-counseling agencies often offer free short seminars or informational brochures on how to get out of debt, manage money, save for a down payment on a house, save for retirement, and so on. They do this as a service to the community, like any nonprofit agency may do.

If you're not ready to speak to a counselor but want more information, consider attending one of these seminars. There you'll meet one or more of the counselors who work for the agency, and you may become more comfortable with the idea of confiding in this perfect stranger. Credit counselors are listed in the Yellow Pages and on the Internet.

Consolidating Your Debt

Instead of writing a separate check for the minimum amount to all of your creditors, all of that unsecured debt (debt that doesn't have a sellable item, like a house or a car, attached to it) can be turned into one payment—usually at a much lower interest rate—that you can more easily manage each month. This is what debt consolidation is all about.

Debt consolidation is not a loan, nor is it a forgiveness of your debts: You do pay off all your debts in due time. But debt consolidation often offers a lower interest rate than you're currently being charged, and if your debts are with collection agencies who expect immediate payment, you may be able to take more time to pay those debts. The best part? The harassing phone calls and letters will stop immediately.

Usually, you sign an agreement in which you allow your credit counselor to contact your creditors, let your counselor submit a budget on your behalf, agree to make your new payment on time (or have your payments automatically withdrawn from your checking or savings account), and agree not to get into further debt. If your creditors agree (and they usually do), you are usually in a position to be free of these debts in three to six years, provided your budget allows for this. Your credit counselor will put you on a tight budget until your debt is paid off.

Using an Accredited Agency

Most, but not all, debt consolidation is performed by credit-counseling agencies. Before you sign on with any agency, check with the Council on Accreditation of Services for Families and Children, the National Foundation for Credit Counseling, and the Better Business Bureau. Information on these agencies is in Appendix A.

Remember that not all credit counselors are the same! Credit card companies have always appreciated credit-counseling services that help people figure out how to pay back their debts, even if it takes them a long time. This is because when cardholders file for the alternative—bankruptcy—the credit card companies often get no payment at all. So, to help these non-profits, credit card companies sometimes donate a percentage of the card balance to the credit-counseling service. Some entrepreneurs, hungry for the fee that credit card companies give for credit counseling, have started for-profit businesses that advertise as credit counselors. But these companies often push the consumer to pay the credit card companies first—or worse, will work only with debts owed to creditors that pay them—which may not be in your best interest.

Examining the Fee—if Any—for Debt Consolidation

Most nonprofits charge a nominal fee for debt consolidation. Expect this, but do not pay more than $25 per month for this service. The money goes to a good cause—paying the agency's considerable expenses—and because of your lower interest rates, you'll still save a bundle of money.

Reviewing the Terms of Your Agreement

Be sure you read the terms of your agreement carefully. You'll usually be expected to make your monthly payment on time—with no exceptions—and you'll also agree not to get into any more debt. This is a bit of tough love because, ultimately, you can't break your cycle of debt if your credit-counseling agency bails you out and then you get right back into debt again. Because they're going to all the trouble of intervening on your behalf, you have to agree to change your lifestyle. It's a tall order, but it's the only way most credit-counseling agencies will work.

Consolidating Your Debts on Your Own

Another way to consolidate your debts is to use one of your credit cards to pay off all your other debts. Many credit cards even provide checks or special forms that help simplify this process.

Under most circumstances, however, consolidating this way—on your own and without the guidance and support of a counselor—isn't a good idea. Because you won't have signed an agreement not to rack up any more debt, you may be tempted to use your now-paid-off credit cards to spend more money, making your situation worse.

In addition, even if one of your credit cards is offering a low interest rate to transfer the balances from your other cards to theirs, the rate is usually good only for a limited amount of time (like six months) and may skyrocket after that. Many credit cards also charge a transaction fee to pay off the balances of other cards. A credit counselor can usually arrange for an even lower interest rate for your debts—and it won't expire.

Selling Some Assets

Besides debt consolidation, there is another way to raise money to pay off your debts: Sell some of your assets. If your house, apartment, storage unit, or parent's house is stocked with items belonging to you that you no longer use and that may have some resale value, consider selling them and using the money to pay down your debts.

ESSENTIAL

Don't confuse pawnshops with tag sales, where you drag out all your stuff and try to make a few bucks. Let's be clear: The people who run pawnshops are nearly always loan sharks, often charging as much as a 25 percent annual interest rate. Steer clear!

Selling Valuable Items

Items that you may be able to sell—and that may be valuable—include furniture, jewelry, an automobile or motorcycle, exercise equipment, recreational toys (pool table, bike), paintings, signed books, computer equipment, guns, memorabilia (baseball cards, signed sports balls), coin or stamp collections, and outdoor equipment (grill, riding mower).

Whatever items you plan to sell, if you expect a high price for them, make sure they're in excellent condition. If they're not nearly new, consider holding a tag sale (see the following section).

Don't sell any items that don't belong to you! That may be considered theft, landing you in hot water. Also, don't sell anything that has a loan against it unless you plan to pay off the loan that same day. Contact your lender about how to sell an item that they hold a lien against.

You can sell valuable items in a variety of ways:

- **Advertise in your local newspaper or a pay-only-if-you-sell publication.** Although an ad in your local paper can be a bit pricey, you won't have to mess with shipping the item to an out-of-town buyer. Classified ads in some papers are quite inexpensive—and most feature a searchable Internet component. The pay-when-you-sell publications, either online or in print form, allow you to advertise for free until you sell the item, at which time you pay a percentage of the selling price—sometimes as much as 15 percent. This option is a good idea if you're not sure your item will sell.
- **Visit a reputable dealer in antiques, paintings, guns, jewelry, books, coins, or stamps.** If you think your item has some value, see a dealer who resells the type of item you wish to sell. Don't visit a pawnshop or any other shady business. Go to the best, highest-class dealer you can find and present your item for sale. If you aren't satisfied with the price, go elsewhere. That particular dealer may simply have too many of what you're trying to sell; another dealer may not.
- **Auction off the item, either online or with a service in your community.** Your items will have to be fairly valuable to others to warrant a live auction (call your local auction company to arrange an appraisal), but even inexpensive items can be auctioned via online services like eBay (*www.eBay.com*).

If you choose an option that will require you to send an item to another city or state (and this is usually the case with online auction services), make sure you find out how much FedEx or UPS will charge you to send your item, insured, via one- or two-day service. Add that cost to your base price. Also, do not send your item without first receiving payment: Either send it C.O.D. or require payment from the buyer before sending the item.

Many online auction services now use a third-party escrow company that receives the money from the buyer and holds it until you send the item and it's received in good condition. The escrow company then sends you the money, charging you or the buyer or both of you a fee in the process.

Holding a Tag Sale

If you own a lot of items, but none is of much value, consider holding a tag sale (also called a yard sale or garage sale). Although your items will sell for much less than you paid for them, you may be able to make hundreds of dollars selling items you consider to be junk. Don't forget, however, that lugging all your items out to the garage or yard, marking them with prices, and being anchored to your sale for a day or two is time-consuming and challenging!

Be sure to mark the price on every single item and include a range of prices, from twenty-five cents for old kitchen towels to $40 for a dresser that's in good condition. This will keep your buyers happy.

To attract customers, set out an attention-grabber—an item that's highly unusual or brightly colored—near the end of your driveway. Make your sale seem full by pulling some of your larger items out of the garage into the driveway. If you don't think you have enough stuff to attract attention, consider combining a sale with neighbors, friends, or family.

Don't include your phone number in the ad—you'll spend the day of the sale on the phone, distracted from helping your buyers and spotting shoplifters.

Be sure to advertise your sale in your local newspaper. For a fee (generally $10–$25), your sale will be advertised a few days in advance (in the paper and online), and you may even receive some signs to place near your house, at intersections, or on busier streets, showing shoppers how to find you. Your ad should include directions, hours, a list of items, and whether you'll hold your sale in the event of rain.

Expect early birds to arrive from sixty to ninety minutes before your posted time. If you're not ready to open, ignore them and reiterate that you'll be opening at the time listed in the paper. Most of these early shoppers are antique or resale-shop dealers who want the pick of your tag-sale litter. If you let them in early, regular folks who saw your ad and thought it'd be fun to go to a garage sale may be furious with you!

Good garage-sale operators get change (a roll of quarters plus small bills) the day before the sale, but if you do this, keep the money box in your hands at all times. A common scam is for one person to distract you while another steals the money box. Also, if you're not good at addition, keep a calculator nearby.

Cashing in Savings Bonds or Stocks

If you own bonds or stocks that aren't earmarked for your (or your child's) education or for your retirement and they are currently valuable, consider cashing them in to pay down your debt. Before deciding, visit your local bank or stockbroker to determine the value of these assets, as well as any penalties and other costs or commissions associated with selling them.

Using Your House to Pay Off Your Debts

Using your home's equity to get out from under crushing debt is very popular today. See Chapter 10 for tips, tricks, and techniques for tapping your home's equity, which is the value of your home minus the mortgage owed on it.

Declaring Bankruptcy

Bankruptcy generally isn't a good idea because, although it probably seems much easier than credit counseling or selling some of your belongings, it can haunt you for a good portion of your life. Think of it this way: Would you ever loan money to a friend who once borrowed it but never paid it back? Neither will lenders, including those that loan money for cars and homes and those that offer unsecured loans like credit cards and store charge cards. You may even have trouble getting the utilities for your house or apartment hooked up if you've declared bankruptcy. (This means you'll have to prepay these services until you establish a good payment record.) In addition, many stores and other companies won't accept checks from you if you've recently declared bankruptcy.

Chapter 10

Refinancing Your Home and Tapping Your Equity

Your house may be a source of riches or a money pit, depending on how well you take advantage of the refinancing options available to you. In addition, if you choose to tap the equity that has built up in your home, you may be able to pay off your existing debt. This chapter shows you how.

10

Finding Money in Your Home

When you think of finding money in your home, you probably think of those pennies and dimes that find their way under the cushions of your couch. Or perhaps you think of the hideous painting your uncle left you that's sure to be worth millions at an auction.

But the real trick to finding money in your house is to understand how to reduce your monthly mortgage payment (which is probably your largest financial obligation each month) and/or tap your equity. This chapter explains the process from top to bottom. If you don't own a home, you may not find this chapter very useful—but you may want to move on to Chapter 17 to find out what's involved in buying a new-to-you house.

Refinancing Your House

If interest rates are lower than they were when you bought your existing house, and if you plan to stay in your house for at least two more years, consider refinancing. When you refinance, you stay in your current house but get a new loan at a lower interest rate than you got on your first mortgage. Ideally, you want to keep the same number of years in your new mortgage as you have left on your old one.

While you want to shop around for the best refinancing interest rates, also shop around for closing costs—the costs associated with sealing the deal on your refinancing. Your current lender may have a slightly higher interest rate than other lenders, but may not charge you for a new inspection, new credit report, and so on. Keep in mind, too, that you can often roll these costs into your mortgage.

When you refinance, many lenders will offer you cash to pay off your credit card debt, to take a vacation, or to spend on whatever you feel like buying, using the equity in your home (the amount your house is worth minus the amount you owe). If your debts are crushing you, you may decide to use the equity to pay them off and start with a clean slate (see the following section). But if you would use that money for anything other than getting rid of large amounts of high-interest debt, don't succumb to this sneaky trick on the part of lenders. They just want your loan to be bigger so they can make more money. But you want your loan to be smaller—both in terms of monthly payments and the number of years before you pay it off—so don't ever take this option unless you're absolutely sure you will use the cash effectively.

Remember that refinancing your car or house doesn't mean you shirk your financial responsibility on these loans. Instead, by locking in a lower interest rate than you originally borrowed at, you can either reduce your monthly payments or keep the same monthly payments and reduce the length of your loan.

Many people ask how much lower than your current interest rate your new mortgage interest rate has to be to make refinancing attractive. Some say the rule is two percentage points. Others say that even half a percentage point can make a difference for some mortgages. To find out how much difference one percentage point can make, visit *www.smartmoney.com* and follow the links to Personal Finance, Real Estate, The Mortgage Calculator. (If you don't have a computer, take a trip to your local library to use its Internet service.) There you'll find just about the coolest mortgage calculator ever invented. Type in your mortgage information, and you can see the impact of changing not only the interest rate, but also any extra payments you might want to make each month (under the prepayments section), lump-sum payments (like putting a bonus from work toward your mortgage), changing the length of the mortgage, and so on.

Understanding Equity

Equity is the portion of your house that you own, mortgage-free. You can calculate your equity as follows:

1. **Determine the current value of your home.** This amount may be higher, and in some cases, *much* higher, than the amount you paid for it. The value may also be lower than what you paid if the house was overvalued

when you bought it or if the real-estate market in your area has slumped. A mortgage company requires an appraisal, done by a professional, to determine this value, but you can guess, based on what homes in your neighborhood have been selling for.

2. **Determine the current payoff on your mortgage.** If you don't receive a monthly statement or receipt that tells you the payoff amount, call your mortgage company and ask for it.
3. **Subtract the payoff from the current value.** This is the equity in your home.

Instead of calculating the current value of your home, some lenders use the value when you bought the home. If that was more than a couple of years ago, the current value may be much higher.

Refinancing Your Home and Taking Out Equity

Refinancing your home and turning some of the equity in your home into cash is a logical way to ease your current debt load. Refinancing is simply financing your mortgage again in an attempt to decrease your monthly payments, the interest rate of your mortgage, the length of your loan, or all three.

Suppose your house is worth $170,000, you financed $153,000, and you currently owe $120,000. Your equity is $50,000. If you refinance without touching the equity, your new loan will be for $120,000, which will make your payments lower than when you bought the house. And if interest rates are lower than when you first obtained your mortgage, your payments will be lower still. You can then decide whether you want to decrease the length of your loan (say, from thirty years to fifteen) while keeping the same monthly payment as before, or whether you want to keep the length of the loan the same and have a lower debt obligation every month.

You can, however, also use some of the equity in your house to pay off other debts. Refinancing and removing equity at the same time amounts to getting a new loan for a higher amount than you currently owe on your home. Instead of refinancing your home for $120,000, you can receive cash for some portion of your equity—perhaps $15,000—and refinance for $135,000 ($120,000 owed on your mortgage plus $15,000 cash).

FACT

Not all of the equity in your home will be available for you to cash in. Some lenders require you to keep 20 to 25 percent of your home's value as an ongoing down payment. Other lenders don't allow you to use the current value of your home, and instead use the original purchase price to determine your equity.

Do You Have Enough Equity?

If you bought your house with a 3-percent down payment on a thirty-year loan four years ago, and your house hasn't increased much in value, you may not have enough equity to tap. Thirty-year loans are notorious for building equity very slowly. In fact, if you finance $100,000 on a thirty-year loan at 7 percent with $5,000 down, you'll have paid just $4,400 of your $100,000 mortgage after four years, and only $13,600 after ten years. On an identical loan for fifteen years, though, you'll have chewed up almost $17,000 of your mortgage after four years, and nearly $53,000 after ten years.

Before applying for a refinance with cash back, make sure you have enough equity. Keep in mind, however, that when interest rates are lower than they were for your original loan, you should still consider refinancing without cashing out any of your equity, either to lower your monthly payments and relieve some of your monthly debt or to reduce your mortgage to fifteen years, allowing you more options for saving for retirement or your child's college education.

Do You Have a Solid Retirement Plan?

This may seem like an odd question in a chapter about tapping your home's equity. If your retirement years are well provided for, either by your company's retirement plan or by investments you've made, lowering the equity in your house by refinancing and getting cash back is a fine idea. But if your retirement savings is shaky or nonexistent, keep the equity in your house and refinance for the fewest number of years possible.

You can sell your large home and move to a smaller one when you retire, paying cash for the smaller home and putting the difference into your retirement fund. See Chapter 21 for more on saving for your retirement.

If you refinance your home for fifteen years when you're forty years old, you'll own your home free and clear when you're fifty-five. You'll realize two benefits: You can spend the ten years from fifty-five to sixty-five putting the amount of your previous house payment into retirement savings *and* you won't have house payments when you retire, which means you'll need less retirement income.

Qualifying for Refinancing

Whether you refinance with or without taking out some of the equity in your home, you want to make sure the refinancing meets the conditions in the following sections.

You Must Have Good Credit

Your credit rating is a reflection of how responsibly you've used credit and paid your bills over the years. If you're interested in refinancing your home but have poor—or even moderate—credit, you may want to wait a year or two while improving your credit rating. A poor credit rating is usually the result of the following, and it can be improved in the following ways:

- **High debt-to-income ratio.** Your new house payment should take up no more than 28 percent of your monthly income; your total financial obligations (mortgage payment, insurance, car and credit card payments, utilities) should total no more than 36 percent of your monthly income. To improve your debt-to-income ratio, you'll need to pay off and/or reduce some of your financial obligations or increase your income.

- **Late payments.** If you have a history of paying any of your bills—especially your mortgage payments—after they're due, you're likely to be denied a new mortgage. To deal with this problem, spend at least a year paying every single one of your bills early or on time, and then apply for a refinanced mortgage. In your application, include a letter stating your new commitment to cleaning up your poor payment history and explaining your diligence over the previous year.

- **Too much credit.** If you apply for every charge card or store credit card offer you receive, you may struggle in your refinancing plans. Having too much credit, even if you don't use it, worries lenders because if you should choose to max those charge cards, you might have trouble making your mortgage payments. To compensate for this potential setback, immediately cancel all but two of your credit cards and store-charge cards and don't apply for any new credit.

Under the Fair Credit Reporting Act, you're allowed to receive one free credit report every twelve months. Go to *www.annualcreditreport.com* or call 877-322-8228.

You can also contact each of the three major credit bureaus individually: Experian (800-301-7195, *www.experian.com*); Equifax (800-525-6285, *www.equifax.com*); and Trans Union (800-680-7289, *www.transunion.com*). For between $10 and $20, these companies send you a copy of your credit report and credit score so that you can set about improving it, if necessary. (If you are ever denied credit, you can get a free copy of your credit report within sixty days of the application.)

Remember that credit reports can be wrong. To be sure, request a copy of your credit report every year or so and correct (in writing) any mistakes that you see.

Interest Rates and Closing Costs Should Be Low

Before considering any refinancing, make sure the interest rate is low enough to make the charges (which are usually lumped into what's called closing costs) associated with refinancing worthwhile. **WORKSHEET 10-1** helps you determine how much money refinancing will save you (or cost you!)— you'll need to use a loan calculator like the one at *www.smartmoney.com* (click on Personal Finance, Real Estate, The Mortgage Calculator).

WORKSHEET 10-1
Financing and Closing Costs

Current mortgage amount (total owed)		$
Closing costs (if added into loan amount)	+	$
Total new mortgage amount	=	$
Mortgage rate		$
Approximate new monthly payment (from calculator)	=	$
Monthly escrow	+	$
Total new monthly payment	=	$
Current monthly payment	–	$
Monthly difference*	=	$
Closing costs (if up-front payment is needed)		$

*If this is a positive number, you'll pay more for your new mortgage.

Escrow is an account that mortgage companies usually create for you when you have a low-down-payment mortgage: One-twelfth of your annual homeowner's insurance and property taxes is added to your mortgage payment. The mortgage company then pays your insurance and taxes from the escrow account when those payments are due. Putting your tax and insurance money into an escrow account may seem convenient, but it costs you a bundle of money in the interest that you could be earning on that money throughout the year.

If you're refinancing, try to keep 20 to 25 percent equity so that you don't have to contribute to an escrow account. You don't want to continue paying escrow if you don't have to.

If you're currently paying escrow and have paid down 20 to 25 percent of your purchase price, ask your mortgage company to terminate your escrow account and send you a check for the balance. You can then deposit your insurance and tax payments into a savings account, out of which you pay those annual or semiannual costs yourself.

Understanding Home Equity Lines of Credit

Applying for a home equity line of credit is similar to—but much simpler than—refinancing your home. Instead of refinancing, which can include expensive closing costs, you simply apply for a line of credit against the equity in your home (see the preceding section for the lowdown on equity and how much is enough). A line of credit is like a loan, but instead of getting cash or a check from the lender, you get a checkbook to spend your equity on anything you want. If you write checks from that account (to yourself or anyone else), the line of credit is considered activated, and you must pay at least the minimum loan payment, an amount that repays the check(s) you've written in about ten years. The more checks you write, the higher your payment will be. Using the account also lowers your equity in your home until you pay the loan back.

The following sections help you determine the advantages and disadvantages associated with home equity lines of credit. In addition, **WORKSHEET 10-2** helps you decide whether a home equity line of credit is right for you.

Advantage: You Can Pay Off Debts with a Lower-Rate Loan

Although home equity lines of credit carry an interest rate that's usually about two percentage points higher than your primary mortgage interest rate, if you use the line to pay off high-interest credit card debt, you'll save a bundle.

ALERT!

Most lenders change their home equity line of credit interest rates daily or weekly. You might write a check when the interest rate is 6 percent and end up paying it off for several years at 8 or 10 percent. For this reason, plan to repay your line of credit as soon as possible after tapping it.

Advantage: Interest Is Probably Tax Deductible

The interest on your line of credit is usually tax deductible if you itemize—just like the interest on your mortgage payment is tax deductible. If you're paying less in taxes, you are, in a sense, lowering your interest rate even more. See Chapter 17 for more on the tax advantages of owning your home.

Advantage: Applying Is a Cinch When You Buy or Refinance Your Home

If you're applying for a new mortgage or are refinancing, you can often apply for a home equity line of credit at the same time. This eliminates duplicating the loan-application paperwork and fees associated with applying for a loan (such as paying for your credit report).

Advantage: You Can Plan Ahead

If you know that your income is going to drop in the future, you can apply for a home equity line of credit long before this drop in income happens. Even though you won't be as good a credit risk after you reduce your income, you'll still have the home equity line of credit locked in and can use it if you need to.

Disadvantage: Annual Fees Can Be High

Some lenders charge annual fees of $20 to $150 for home equity lines of credit. Be sure to figure that amount into your calculations if you're planning to pay off a high-interest-rate debt with your home equity line of credit.

Some lenders offer periodic "sales" on annual fees for home equity lines of credit. If annual fees are too high for you, ask whether the fees will ever be discounted, perhaps during a slow month for applications or when you open a checking or savings account with the lender.

Disadvantage: Two Mortgage Payments

If you're using a home equity line of credit to pay off existing high-interest debt (like credit cards), your monthly payment for the home equity line of credit will most likely be lower than for the high-interest debt, due to the lower interest rate and the relatively long life of the loan (usually ten years).

But if you're going to use the money to make improvements to your home or for any other new financial obligation, you'll have two monthly house payments instead of one, although the home equity line of credit payment is likely to be much lower than the payment for your primary mortgage. If you want to make only one payment, you'll have to refinance and take equity out of your home.

Disadvantage: You Must Have Enough Equity Available in Your Home

In order to get a home equity line of credit, you must have equity available in your home. After all, you're borrowing against the equity, and if you don't have much, you don't have anything to borrow against. Your home equity line of credit, then, will only be as large as your available equity, minus whatever down-payment amount the lender expects you to maintain with them (and that can be as much as 25 percent—check with your lender).

Disadvantage: You Lower the Equity in Your Home

If you're planning to use your home as part of your retirement plan, using a home equity line of credit will reduce your ability to do that. The more you tap into your equity, the less you'll receive in cash when you sell your house.

Disadvantage: You Must Own Your Own Home

You must own (or have a mortgage on) your own home in order to qualify for a home-equity line of credit. Even if you've been living in your grandmother's home and have made all the payments on it, if the house isn't in your name, you can't get a home-equity line of credit.

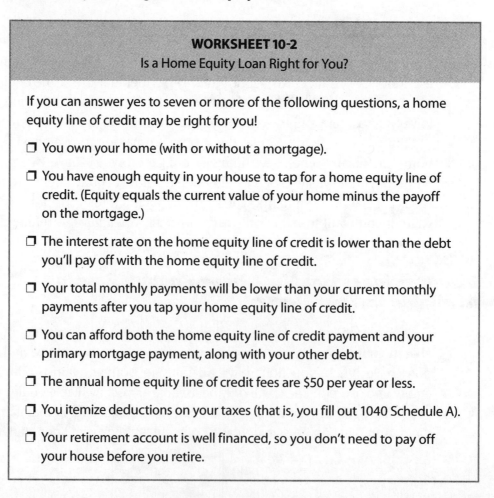

WORKSHEET 10-2
Is a Home Equity Loan Right for You?

If you can answer yes to seven or more of the following questions, a home equity line of credit may be right for you!

❐ You own your home (with or without a mortgage).

❐ You have enough equity in your house to tap for a home equity line of credit. (Equity equals the current value of your home minus the payoff on the mortgage.)

❐ The interest rate on the home equity line of credit is lower than the debt you'll pay off with the home equity line of credit.

❐ Your total monthly payments will be lower than your current monthly payments after you tap your home equity line of credit.

❐ You can afford both the home equity line of credit payment and your primary mortgage payment, along with your other debt.

❐ The annual home equity line of credit fees are $50 per year or less.

❐ You itemize deductions on your taxes (that is, you fill out 1040 Schedule A).

❐ Your retirement account is well financed, so you don't need to pay off your house before you retire.

Chapter 11

Adding Income

If you've reduced your expenses as much as you can and still have trouble finding the money to reach your financial goals, consider temporarily or permanently adding to your income and putting that money toward your debts or into savings.

Recognizing What Additional Work Can Mean for You

Extra work can be both a blessing and a curse. Extra income can help you pay off nagging debts that you just can't seem to get anywhere with any other way. Working a second job can also help you build new skills that could lead to a different full-time job or a new business of your own. And nearly anyone can put up with a crazy schedule for a few weeks or even a couple of months, especially if you know exactly when the long hours will end and can count down the days—and add up your extra income.

But managing a heavy workload isn't easy. You have to juggle your responsibilities at home, your relationships with the people who are important to you, and your need for rest and relaxation with your new requirements on the job.

E ALERT!

Before trading in your time for money, be sure you can't cut back on your expenses enough to gain the extra money you need. Chapters 5 though 10 give you tips and tricks for reducing your monthly financial obligations. Consider adding income only as a last resort.

The following sections help you define the pluses and minuses of additional work, and give you some tips for smoothing the rough road ahead.

New Skills That May Lead to Different Work

One approach to choosing your second job is to look for one that builds your skills in a way that will help further your career. Suppose, for example, that you don't have any computer skills at all. You see an advertisement for a job that requires fifteen hours of work each week at your local library reshelving books. But you also know that the library's checkout system is completely computerized, so at your interview, you ask whether you would be able to spend a few hours a week learning the system and, at some point, helping patrons use the system, too. Within just a few months, you may develop enough computer skills to be able to update your resume and apply for a completely different day job—one that requires a basic knowledge of computers—with your current employer or with a new one.

A Foundation for Starting Your Own Company

If you're hoping to go into business for yourself and want extra income to pay off debts before you start the company, or as a cushion against uncertain income, you can start your business on a very part-time basis—perhaps on evenings and weekends—and build both a client base and a reputation before you go into the business full time.

Suppose, for example, you're thinking of starting a landscaping company. Using the additional evening daylight hours in the summer months, you could begin your landscaping business during evenings and weekends. Let your coworkers, friends, and neighbors know about your new business, and let word spread about your great product or service. As your business picks up, you can begin to cut down your hours at your other job or quit that job altogether.

ALERT!

If your new business will compete with the company you work for, take extra care. Don't advertise at work and be sure never to use your company's equipment or ideas for your own business. And never work for yourself when you're on company time.

Besides landscaping, some business ideas that might lend themselves to evenings and weekends include catering, photography, graphic design, Web site design, furniture refinishing and repair, selling antiques, home remodeling and repair, closet and room organizing, dog training, tutoring, selling cosmetics, and so on. This is by no means an exhaustive list—see the "Starting a Small Business" section at the end of this chapter for more information on getting started running your own company.

Far Less Available Time

The hours you spend working more will have to come from somewhere. Unless you have hours and hours of unfilled free time right now, your additional work is probably going to keep you from spending time with your family, running errands, exercising, futzing with your house or car, visiting friends and extended family, taking a vacation, working on your hobby, reading, playing with your pets, and so on. This isn't trivial—remember the saying, "All work and no play makes Jack a dull boy"? Working too much can dull your senses, making life seem as though it revolves around work, when, in fact, a healthy life revolves around the people and events that make you happy.

Always include your family in your plans to work additional hours. Not only will they miss spending time with you, they'll probably also be asked to pick up some of your chores around the house, so they deserve to be included from the start.

If you're planning to add extra income for a short time—say, until your $6,500 credit card debt is paid off—you can plan ahead with friends and family, agreeing, perhaps, that they'll help you by running some of your errands while you're working to pay off this debt. You may also be able to agree that as soon as the debt is paid off, you'll quit earning the extra income and immediately spend more time with them, maybe even by taking a well-deserved vacation. Although the thought of extending your extra income indefinitely may seem like a wise financial choice, keep in mind that life isn't all about work—if you do nothing but work and make money, you'll be likely to either lose the valuable parts of your life or burn out on your existing jobs and begin to dread them.

If you're planning to add extra income for a longer time—perhaps taking on a higher-paying job that requires far more working hours—try to find ways to gain back some of your free time. Move closer to work, hire someone to help with errands and chores, exercise or meet with friends before work or during your lunch hour, listen to books on tape while you drive, take fun vacations, and so on. Then when you are home, be fully in the moment, not working, thinking about work, or preparing for the next day of work.

If you're adding work temporarily—for a few weeks or months—you can probably survive this additional stress without damaging your health or relationships. But if you plan to continue to work a lot, find ways to reduce stress and continue to connect with those around you.

Added Stress

Working too much taxes you physically and emotionally, and that can make you fatigued, subject to illness and injury, and irritable, none of which makes you a very good companion, parent, or friend. In addition, if your work is highly mental in nature, you may suffer mental stress that can rob you of your ability to converse intelligently and work on detailed hobbies or other projects during your down time.

Higher Taxes

Ben Franklin said that "a penny saved is a penny earned." Technically, though, he should have said that a penny saved is about 1.20 cents earned, because taxes can eat up that much (or more) of your earnings. If, on your current income, you can find a way to cut $10 from your expenses, you'll have $10 more to put toward paying off debt, into savings, into your retirement account, and so on. But if you work more, you'll have to earn between $12.50 and $13.25, which will get you about $10 after taxes, to pay off $10 from your debt or add it to your savings account.

Because of taxes, it's always more efficient to make the same income— or even to make less income—and cut your expenses than it is to add more income. Using the tax calculator at *www.freedom.gov* (and then following the links to Tax Relief Info, then Tax Calculator), fill out **WORKSHEET 11-1** to see just how taxes take a bite out of your extra income.

WORKSHEET 11-1
Does Extra Income Equal Extra Taxes?

Income	Total Taxes Due
Current	$
+ $500	$
+ $1,000	$
+ $2,000	$
+ $3,000	$
+ $5,000	$
+ $10,000	$
+ $15,000	$
+ $20,000	$
+ $25,000	$
+ $30,000	$

Changing Jobs

One of the simplest ways to increase your income is to look for a new full-time job. In fact, many job counselors advise their clients to look for new work every few years as a way to boost their income (and increase their contacts within the industry). If you receive a 3–5 percent raise every year at your current job, you'll have to work about two to three and a half years before your income goes up by 10 percent. But you may be able to get a 10 percent raise next month by getting a job at another company.

One way to boost your income by staying at your existing job is to change shifts. Often, the third shift (which usually runs from somewhere between 10:00 P.M. and midnight to 6:00 A.M.–8:00 A.M.) pays much more per hour—even as much as fifty cents or a dollar more.

If you do change jobs, however, be sure the new job—with its higher income—doesn't end up costing you more. It could, if the new job is ten miles farther away, requires expensive clothing that must be dry-cleaned, doesn't offer free parking, requires that you carry a cell phone or laptop computer at your cost, and so on. Before accepting a job offer, ask detailed questions about your new responsibilities and the costs that may be involved. If your new job is with your existing company, don't shy away from asking these same questions. Different departments within large corporations often require different dress codes and standard equipment.

Getting a Second Job

Getting a second job can help boost your income, and can be fun at the same time. To make it as enjoyable as possible, try to find work that suits your personality and interests. If, for example, you have a great love of photography or athletics, consider getting a second job at a camera shop or at an athletics store or gym. If you tend to be outgoing, try to find work that allows you to interact with people. If you're shy, consider working behind the scenes at a company that interests you, instead of having to work with people. By matching your personality and interests to your second job, the extra work may not seem as difficult to endure.

ALERT!

Don't let your employee discount get you further into debt. If you work at a camera shop and find yourself buying thousands of dollars worth of equipment that you wouldn't normally have purchased, your second job could be little more than a new way to get into debt.

One of the best times to find a second job in retail is during the holidays. Companies hire seasonal employees from the week of Thanksgiving through the New Year. At that point, you're usually out of a second job, but if you've worked out well for the company and express interest in continuing to work for them, you may be called back for the next holiday season and at various times throughout the year.

Working Overtime

Unless you are a salaried employee who is expected to work as many hours as necessary to complete your work, you may have opportunities to work overtime at your current job to earn additional income.

One of the best perks of working overtime is that you're usually eligible to receive more pay per hour for hours over forty per week—sometimes as much as time and a half or double time. That can add up to a lot of additional income in just a short amount of time.

Whatever you do, don't count on overtime income for your everyday expenses! Companies are notorious for eliminating all overtime work whenever the economy contracts a little bit. You may be told that you'll be earning extra income for six months, only to find the work eliminated six weeks into your stint.

Be aware of the overtime commitments that your company may require, however. Some companies expect you to commit to working overtime for a set period, even six months or a year, before they'll allow you to sign on. And the time required may be open-ended, so that you're getting home at 6:30 P.M. one day and 8:00 P.M. the next. Before accepting this opportunity for additional income, be sure you're clear on exactly what's involved.

Freelancing for Your Own Company

Although freelancing is similar to working overtime because you're doing work outside of your normal working hours for the company you already work for, it's a little different. In general, freelancing involves taking on a project that no one within the company has the time (or the expertise) to complete. It can involve projects from typing a handwritten manuscript or sewing a banner to creating a graphics-heavy company brochure or catering a company event. You work on the project in your spare time, usually on your own equipment at home.

- Freelancing allows you to use your unique skills and talents to earn extra money.
- Freelancing on a particular project doesn't lock you into working extra hours for an indefinite period of time.
- Freelancing can improve your reputation with your current employer, especially if you're able to come through on a difficult or time-sensitive project.
- Freelancing can spin off into a full-time gig if you're able to find more clients in addition to your current employer.

Starting a Small Business

Starting a small, home-based business is one of the hottest trends in the United States today, but it doesn't have to be a full-time investment if you don't want it to be. If you're trying to find a way to earn extra cash but want some control over how and when you work, starting a small business from your home might be just what you're looking for. The following sections help you answer some important questions about starting a part-time business. WORKSHEET 11-2 can help you determine whether earning extra money by starting a small business is right for you.

WORKSHEET 11-2
Business Expenses

Expense	One-Time Costs	Monthly Costs
	$	$
	$	$
	$	$
	$	$
	$	$
	$	$
	$	$
TOTAL:	$	$

Finding the Best Small Business for You

The best small business for you is the one that you're enthusiastic and passionate about. This means that your business idea has to mesh with your skills, unique qualities, and personality. If, for example, you're thinking about starting a catering business but don't really enjoy cooking, you probably won't succeed. If, on the other hand, you've always loved cosmetics and like dealing with people one-on-one, you might want to try your hand as a Mary Kay consultant or Arbonne representative.

Matching your work to your personality, qualities, and skills is the topic of hundreds of books. If you're unsure which business idea will work best for you, take a trip to your local bookstore or library and find one that offers self-tests and ideas about home-based businesses.

ESSENTIAL

If you're planning to start your business part time to earn extra money, be sure you choose one that doesn't require a large commitment of time or a large investment of cash. Although you may turn your business into full-time work sometime in the future, you don't want to jeopardize your current job by taking on more than you can handle.

Determining Whether You're Passionate about Your Business Idea

Finding out whether you're passionate about a business idea is pretty simple—just decide whether you agree or disagree with this statement:

Now that I've come up with a potential business, the thought of not pursuing it seems impossible.

If you agree, you're plenty passionate. But if you disagree; that is, if you think your business concept is just okay or seems like too much work, don't bother pursuing it—you won't have the energy required to make it succeed.

Estimating Your Potential Income and Expenses

Estimating your potential income and expenses is always difficult. To keep the number realistic, come up with three scenarios for both income and expenses: Best case; average case; and worst case. If, for example, you think you can get three catering jobs per month, use that as your best case, but also figure out how much you'll make with just two catering jobs (average case) or one (worst case). Do the same with your income. If you're planning to offer graphic-design services from your home and will rely heavily on a desktop computer and color laser printer, figure in the cost of paper, toner cartridges, and software updates in your best-case scenario. Also figure in repair expenses on that equipment in your worst-case scenario.

Keep in mind that many small-business owners underestimate how much expenses really cost. If you're running a business part time, you may not need to get a second phone number or buy elaborate equipment. On the other hand, you may find that you need to set up a Web site, buy some basic office equipment, invest in business equipment, get inventory for your business, secure a booth at a local antiques mall, and so on. Use **WORKSHEET 11-2** to estimate your business expenses.

Whatever equipment will be essential to your business's success, include it in your worst-case scenario.

Keeping Your Overhead Low

After you think of all the possible equipment you'll need to make your business a success, determine which items would just be nice, which are absolutely necessary, and which you can buy secondhand. Too many first-time business owners spend hundreds or thousands of dollars outfitting their offices, only to find that those expenses don't increase business traffic one bit!

Use the basic principles in this book to create a separate budget just for your business. Make sure that you include all the "hidden costs"—don't underestimate the cost of things like stamps, envelopes, and other incidentals that can really add up in a business.

Suppose you decide that you don't need a fancy desk for your office—a small wooden one will do just fine. You read the classifieds and look through sale flyers from office-equipment stores and find one that's just $75. That's a few hundred less than a new desk would cost, so it's a good deal, right? Not if you're planning to run a business that doesn't require a desk! If you can do your paperwork at the kitchen table, don't bother buying a desk until you find that you really need one.

Understanding Business Taxes

Too many small businesses have folded because their owners failed to estimate their taxes properly. The federal government (and, possibly, your state government, too) requires you to pay approximately one quarter of the taxes your business will owe for the year's income at four separate times throughout the year: April 15, June 15, September 15, and January 15. This is known as the "pay as you go" system.

In order to make these tax payments, you'll need to estimate how much you'll owe in taxes at the end of the year, divide that amount by four, and send a check for that amount by each due date. If you fail to do so, you may have to pay a penalty when you submit your next tax return. Estimating these taxes can be a bit tricky, however. The best way to determine how much you'll owe is to do the following:

1. Estimate your income and business expenses for the year.
2. Locate a copy of last year's income-tax forms (or last year's tax software program) for both federal and state taxes.
3. Fill out Schedule C of the federal form 1040 by using your estimated income and business-expense data.
4. Using last year's income (from your and your spouse's jobs) and last year's federal and state income-tax forms, and adding in your business estimates, find out how much more you would have owed last year if your business had been up and running then.
5. Subtract the amount you actually owed from the amount you would have owed if your business had been in operation. This is how much more you estimate your taxes will be this year.
6. Divide that number by four and send that amount on each quarterly due date.

Continuing to use last year's tax-return forms, keep recalculating this number as you go through the year. If your expenses are higher or your income is lower than you thought, you'll pay less in taxes. If your expenses are lower or your income is higher than you anticipated, you'll pay more. Although tax forms change from year to year, using last year's forms will give you a pretty close estimate.

Deciding Whether You're Ready

WORKSHEET 11-3 can help you decide whether running a small business is the right idea for you.

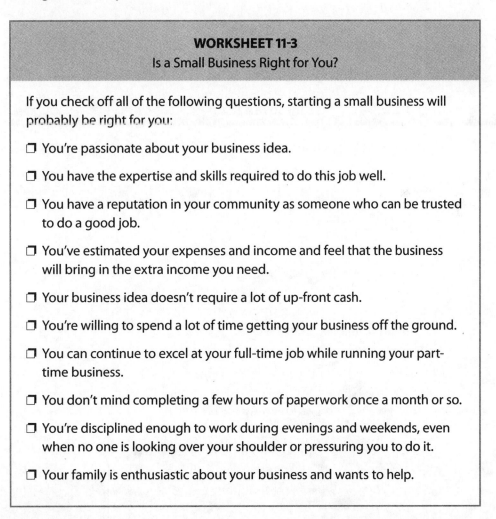

WORKSHEET 11-3
Is a Small Business Right for You?

If you check off all of the following questions, starting a small business will probably be right for you:

❏ You're passionate about your business idea.

❏ You have the expertise and skills required to do this job well.

❏ You have a reputation in your community as someone who can be trusted to do a good job.

❏ You've estimated your expenses and income and feel that the business will bring in the extra income you need.

❏ Your business idea doesn't require a lot of up-front cash.

❏ You're willing to spend a lot of time getting your business off the ground.

❏ You can continue to excel at your full-time job while running your part-time business.

❏ You don't mind completing a few hours of paperwork once a month or so.

❏ You're disciplined enough to work during evenings and weekends, even when no one is looking over your shoulder or pressuring you to do it.

❏ Your family is enthusiastic about your business and wants to help.

Chapter 12

Surviving Unemployment

Losing your job may be the toughest financial blow you'll ever have to take, yet people do survive unemployment; in fact, they often emerge on firmer financial footing (because they've quickly learned to budget and cut back) and with greater confidence in their abilities. This chapter shows you how to move from desperation to success.

Sorting Out Severance Packages and Unemployment Insurance

Your first step should be to assess how much money you may still have coming in—usually from two sources: Severance pay (a lump-sump check from your employer) and unemployment insurance.

Many companies don't offer severance packages, so it's certainly not guaranteed. If the company is laying off employees because it is having financial difficulties, you probably won't be offered any severance pay, but you may be offered a severance package that might include job-placement assistance, continued use of an office so that you still appear to be employed, and freelance opportunities to finish projects that you've been working on. This assistance is not common, however.

If you are offered severance pay, the amount will most likely be based on how long you've worked for the company: A month's pay for every two years worked, for example. If you're offered this pay—six months' worth of income, say—immediately put it away in a safe, interest-bearing account so that it will last you six months (or, perhaps, even longer). If you're not offered any severance, or if the severance pay is so paltry that it runs out before you've even had your resume printed, you're not alone. Sadly, few companies offer this assistance—those that do are usually companies that have recently merged (and, therefore, have a lot of cash) and have laid off a small part of their staff.

If you were fired from your job because of misconduct, unemployment insurance and COBRA-defined coverage will probably not be available to you. These benefits are meant to assist employees who lose their jobs through no fault of their own.

You're far more likely to receive unemployment benefits, however. The moment you hear you've been laid off, call your state's unemployment-insurance agency (you'll find the number in the blue pages or government section of any phone book). While you may have to visit the unemployment office, some states allow you to file a claim by phone or online.

The amount of your unemployment insurance and the length of time you'll receive it is based on how long you've been employed, the state you live in, and the general economic condition in your area. (In times of severe economic downturn, unemployment benefits are often extended for many more weeks than in relatively healthy economic periods.) Your state's unemployment office will know how many weeks you're eligible for and whether you have any chance of having those benefits extended.

As soon as you find another job, your unemployment benefits will stop. Some states, however, have a self-employment assistance plan that encourages you to start your own business. You receive the same benefits as you would if you were looking for work, but instead of sending out resumes and going on interviews, you're spending your time getting your business started. Ask your state whether a self-employment assistance program is available to you.

Locking In Your COBRA-Defined Coverage

The Consolidated Omnibus Budget Reconciliation Act (COBRA) of 1986 was designed to help employees who leave their jobs and are, as a result, without medical insurance coverage. If your former employer had twenty or more employees, COBRA allows you to continue medical insurance coverage for up to eighteen months after leaving your company. The fine print? Well, it's a doozy. You have to pay the entire cost of your insurance—the portion you paid before (it was probably deducted from your salary) and the portion your employer paid on your behalf, which may have run several hundred dollars per month. (Your former employer is also allowed to charge you a 2 percent administration fee.) The coverage you receive—including deductibles and limits on coverage—should be identical to the coverage you had as an employee.

When you're laid off, you should receive information about continuing your medical coverage under COBRA. If you don't receive it, ask for it! You usually have sixty days to elect to continue your coverage (and when you sign up, the coverage is retroactive to your last day on the job) and pay the first payment. If you fail to make the payments, which are usually due monthly, the coverage will be terminated.

Before deciding whether to accept COBRA coverage, call around or search on the Internet for short-term health-care coverage. If you're willing to go with a high-deductible plan (which means that you don't get any benefits until your medical expenses total a ridiculous amount, but you're covered up to a few million dollars if a catastrophe occurs), you may be able to pay hundreds less per month for insurance and still have coverage if a catastrophe occurs. Many conditions, including pre-existing ones and pregnancy, aren't covered (or aren't covered until a year after the policy begins), and a few of these policies can't be renewed after they expire (usually in six to nine months). COBRA's biggest benefit could be that even though it expires eighteen months after you sign on, if you still haven't found work, you're eligible for insurance policies that aren't allowed to exclude pre-existing conditions.

It's no small irony that when you can least afford to pay the entire portion of your medical insurance costs, you have to, in order to continue your coverage. However, if you're tempted to just go without insurance, don't! Doing so may turn a bad financial situation into a catastrophic one.

Seeing to Your Other Insurance Needs

If you're able to lock in COBRA insurance for the next eighteen months, you have one major insurance need taken care of, even if it is frighteningly expensive. But you want to think about your other insurance coverage as well, especially insurance that may have been covered by your employer and insurance that you may be tempted to let lapse while you're unemployed.

Employer-Sponsored Insurance

Your employer may have paid for life, disability, dental, and vision insurance, in addition to medical coverage. Of these, life insurance is the one that's most important to secure while you're unemployed.

Some people think of life insurance as a way to leave great wealth to their children or spouse upon their death, but for most people, life insurance is simply a way to help your family pay for funeral costs and get through a year or so without your income. Many people, therefore, buy enough coverage to pay funeral expenses, pay off the mortgage, and pay for one or two months of income or unemployment benefits. Funeral expenses vary by area—call your local funeral home for an estimate.

You can find out your mortgage balance by calling your mortgage lender and asking for the payoff amount. Use **WORKSHEET** **12-1** to see how large your life-insurance policy should be.

WORKSHEET 12-1
Amount of Life Insurance Needed

Funeral expenses:	$
Mortgage payoff:	$
Monthly income or unemployment benefits:	$
Other amount needed:	$
Other amount needed:	$
Other amount needed:	$
Other amount needed:	$
Other amount needed:	$

Insurance You've Been Paying For

Your employer has probably had nothing to do with your homeowner's or apartment insurance and car insurance. When you're unemployed, you want to keep those insurance policies intact, although this is a good time to shop around for a better price and, if necessary, higher deductibles (see Chapter 7).

Most states won't allow you to let your auto insurance lapse (they'll eventually take away your license plates), and most lenders won't allow you to let your homeowner's insurance lapse (they'll cancel the mortgage and force you to sell your house). Although this may seem intrusive on their part, consider what would happen if you had a fire in your house and didn't carry insurance. The mortgage company wouldn't have a house to sell in order to recoup their loan, so they would make you pay that loan in full immediately. Don't let unemployment go from bad to worse by not maintaining some insurance coverage for your house and car.

ESSENTIAL

You may also have had a retirement plan at your company. For now, don't feel that you need to do anything with this plan, unless you think your company might be in danger of declaring bankruptcy. Otherwise, let it sit until you've had a chance to figure out your next move.

Paring Your Expenses Down to the Bone

Now that you have a sense of what your income might be for the next few weeks and have discovered the cost of paying for your insurance policies, you can create a bare-bones budget that you'll live on until you find your next job.

Your next step is to eliminate every single unnecessary expense so that, even with the increase in medical insurance payments (and, potentially, other insurance premiums, too), you can make your unemployment insurance (plus any savings you may have) last as long as possible.

This is your time to experience living like a monk. Unless you can show directly how spending money will get you another job, put away your credit cards and begin a period of absolutely no discretionary spending. Chapter 2 can help you both with the concept of freezing your spending and with reviewing the information that you'll need for **WORKSHEET 12-2.** Try to see how many of the categories in this worksheet can total zero dollars.

Looking for a Job As Soon As Possible

If your company offers job-hunting assistance, use it, even if it's not the greatest service or assistance available. If nothing else, beginning your job hunt the day after you are laid off doesn't give you much time to worry or get too angry. Both emotions are, of course, perfectly normal reactions to losing your job, but both can also paralyze you. Take the time you need, but if you find yourself unable to get out of bed or unwilling to get off the couch, you may be letting your emotions keep you from getting that next interview.

Looking for a job—especially if you use an office or other location (away from your home) that's been set up for you—gets you out of the house, dressed professionally, and ready to look for your next course in life. In fact, that's often the best approach when job hunting: Treat your job search as though it's your full-time job. Use any facilities your company has provided for you, which may include office space with a telephone, copy machine, computer and printer, resume consultation service, and so on.

If you don't have a top-notch resume and don't have access to any free services that offer resume assistance, take a trip to your local library to review its books on resumes and cover letters, especially those that discuss the best ways to submit them electronically.

If, on the other hand, you aren't offered any job-searching assistance from your company, you can use the same ideas to find your next job. If you need to get out of the house while searching the Internet or newspapers, visit your local library or the FedEx Kinko's copy center in your area. When you do go out, dress professionally and set goals for the day, such as, "I'll find and follow up on three leads today."

WORKSHEET 12-2
A Bare-Bones Budget

Monthly Expense	Amount	Ways to Reduce	New Amount
Groceries and household items	$		$
Day care	$		$
Contributions	$		$
Savings	$		$
Rent on furniture or appliances	$		$
Entertainment/babysitting	$		$
Eating out	$		$
Rent or mortgage	$		$
Car payment or lease	$		$
Electric bill (average)	$		$
Gas bill (average)	$		$
Water bill	$		$
Sewer bill	$		$
Trash pick-up bill	$		$
Cable/DSL/satellite bill	$		$
Telephone bill	$		$
Cell phone bill	$		$
Bank charges	$		$
Haircuts/manicures/pedicures	$		$
Home equity loan	$		$
Other loan	$		$
Credit card or store-charge bill	$		$
Credit card or store-charge bill	$		$
Credit card or store-charge bill	$		$
Credit card or store-charge bill	$		$

WORKSHEET 12-2
A Bare-Bones Budget (*continued*)

Monthly Expense	Amount	Ways to Reduce	New Amount
Credit card or store-charge bill	$		$
Credit card or store-charge bill	$		$
Child support or alimony	$		$
Car maintenance	$		$
House maintenance	$		$
Auto insurance	$		$
Property taxes	$		$
Gifts	$		$
Events to attend	$		$
Clothing and shoes	$		$
Home insurance	$		$
Vehicle registration	$		$
Vacation	$		$
Club membership	$		$
Club membership	$		$
Club membership	$		$
Other:	$		$
Other:	$		$
TOTAL:	$		$

When searching online, search first for job-listing services that are specific to your industry. For more general searches, go to CareerJournal (*www.careerjournal.com*), Monster.com (*www.monster.com*), Yahoo! Hot-Jobs (*www.hotjobs.yahoo.com*), CareerBuilder (*www.careerbuilder.com*), and craigslist (*www.craigslist.org*, and then choose your city). Also, don't forget the classified ads in and Web site for your local paper.

ALERT!

Never pass up the opportunity to network! Although you may prefer that people not know you've lost your job, the people you run into at the coffee house, your daughter's basketball game, or a social gathering with your spouse may be able to help you find your next job.

Starting a Consulting Firm or Small Business

Many laid-off or downsized employees use their misfortune to springboard into a career they've always wanted, as a consultant or small business owner. There are, however, some important points to consider.

Wait to Pursue Big-Business Dreams

If your plans for a business are large in scope—say, you want to open a retail store or open a large consulting firm—being unemployed may not be the best time to establish your business. For a large business that's going to have a lot of overhead (rent, inventory, equipment), you're going to need money, either from a lender or from investors. Unless you received a large severance package or have plenty of money in savings that you could give up as collateral (a guarantee for the lender), you're probably not going to qualify for an influx of cash from a lender or investor while your future is so uncertain. That doesn't mean your big-business plans are impossible, but you'll have a better chance of success if you keep your plans small.

Keep Your Plans Small

Concentrate your self-employment plans on the lowest-overhead business that appeals to you. Plan, for now, to be the only employee (or work with a few other self-employed professionals who also have their own businesses), so that you can eliminate complicated withholding taxes and paperwork and can work out of any spare space in your home. Keep your overhead to a minimum, buying only the items that you absolutely need to run the business. (You can purchase more for your business later, as it grows and prospers.)

Chapter 11 gives you tips on starting a business. The emphasis there is on starting a small business as a means of earning extra income (in addition to your regular job), but much of the information applies to your situation, too.

QUESTION?

How can I get free help with starting my business?
A local office of the Small Business Administration (SBA) offers free seminars, books, and other products to help you get your business off the ground. In addition, the Service Corps of Retired Executives (SCORE) offers free consultations with experienced (and now retired) execs.

Holding Down a Couple of Part-Time Jobs

If you're unable to find a full-time job to replace the one you had, one way to get your financial picture back in focus is to look for a couple of part-time jobs and combine the hours to work full time (or longer). The following sections give you a few tips for successfully managing two part-time jobs. Keep in mind that working long hours can take a toll on you and your family (see Chapter 11).

Make Each Employer Aware of the Other

If your hours aren't fixed at either job, make sure that each employer knows you have another job—and let each employer know what hours you're available to work. You'll have a better chance of making this situation work.

Establish Boundaries

Scheduling two part-time jobs can be extremely difficult unless you establish some boundaries for the hours you work on each job. For example, Job A might be weekday mornings only—anytime from 6:00 A.M. to 1:00 P.M., Monday through Friday. Job B might include weekend hours, from early in the morning until late at night.

You'll still have some conflicts—like when your weekend boss has you working until midnight on Sunday and your weekday boss wants you in at 6:00 A.M. on Monday. But by establishing some boundaries for each job, you'll have less overlap.

Try to Get a Set Weekly Schedule

When you look for part-time work, give priority to jobs that give you the exact same hours each week. That way, you'll be able to work your other part-time job around the first without any overlaps.

Considering Another Geographic Location

If you're struggling to find work in your immediate area, you can always expand your prospects by branching out into another geographic area. This sounds simple, right? Unfortunately, it isn't. Finding out about out-of-town positions is easier than it has ever been, thanks to the Internet. Actually landing the job, however, can be much more difficult. In general, employers in other geographic locations find that out-of-towners are expensive to hire and often flee back to their home area the first chance they get.

The Web sites listed in the "Looking for a Job As Soon As Possible" section earlier in this chapter are easy to use and list thousands of jobs (usually by the dates they were posted, so you always know how hot the lead is). If you're interested in taking on work nearly anywhere in the United States, make a point of checking these sites every morning, searching by city, if possible.

To make yourself a more attractive candidate in the eyes of an out-of-town employer, consider the tips in the following sections.

Clarify That You're Not Expecting Relocation Assistance

The main fear of out-of-town employers is that you're going to expect relocation assistance if they offer you a job. That assistance can include the costs of house hunting in advance of the move, the move itself, help selling your house (including, but not limited to, actually buying your house from you if it doesn't sell), help finding employment for your spouse, paid trips back to tie-up loose ends, and so on.

These costs can be incredibly expensive even for large companies, so put their mind at ease by indicating in your cover letter that you're planning to pay for your own move and will not require any relocation assistance.

Say You'll Pay for Interview Expenses

If you were happily employed and had the leisure of weighing out-of-town job options, you might expect to be flown out for an interview. But given that you want to find work immediately, mention in your cover letter that you plan to pay for your own interview expenses (driving or flying out, staying in a hotel, paying for meals, and so on).

FACT

One way to get out-of-town employers to respond quickly is to let them know that you'll be in the area on a certain date—say, four or six weeks out—and that you'd like to set up an interview at that time. This gives the company a chance to see you in person, but it also forces them to interview you on a timely basis.

Indicate That You're Moving Regardless

Even if you aren't planning to move without a job, make your cover letter sound as if you're definitely relocating to the area and are looking for employment in advance. This, combined with your readiness to pay for your own interview and relocation expenses, may make you as attractive as an in-town candidate.

Be sure to mention all of the non-work-related reasons that you're moving to the area. (Hint: Make up some of these reasons if you don't have any!)

Chapter 13

Sticking to Your Budget in an Emergency

Too often, a budget gets derailed because of an unexpected expense, especially in the first few months. Ideally, you want to keep money in savings for such emergencies, but in case you haven't had time to build up your cash reserves, this chapter gives you ideas for sticking to your budget even in the worst of times.

If Your Car Breaks Down

Most people on a tight budget have one prayer: "Please don't let anything happen to my car." That's because car repairs can cost hundreds or even thousands of dollars, and you often can't get back and forth to work without a car. So what do you do if your car does break down?

Immediately Find a Way to Work

Whether you have to arrange for a ride from a coworker, ride a bike, take the bus, rent a car, or walk, if you're in an accident or your car isn't running, figure out a way to get to and from work without delay. Too many jobs have been lost because, for three or four days, an employee couldn't get to work and an employer wasn't very understanding. If you have to miss or be late for even one day of work because of your car, call your supervisor and explain that you have car problems and are trying to find an alternate way to work right away.

Consider alternate ways to get to and from work before your car breaks down. Even if you never have a bit of trouble with your car, you'll have the peace of mind that comes from knowing how you'd handle a car crisis if you had one.

Research Your Warranty and Insurance Coverage

If you recently bought the car new and your car troubles aren't due to an accident, your car is probably under warranty and will be repaired for free. Even if you bought the car used, you may have a short-term warranty that covers the repairs you need. If your car isn't running because of an accident, call your insurance company to determine how much of the repairs your policy pays for.

Get a Free Repair Estimate

If you can get your car to a repair shop, take it there and ask for a free, no-commitment estimate. Make sure you emphasize the "free" and "no-commitment" parts of the estimate. Many repair shops don't charge for estimates as long as you end up repairing your car there. If you decide not to repair it, or if you go somewhere else for the repair, they'll bill you $50 or $100 for the estimate! Be sure to let the repair shop know that you're on a very tight budget and need to know the least expensive way to get your car running again.

QUESTION?

How do I describe a problem if I don't know anything about cars?
Simply tell the repair shop what sounds you're hearing as you drive (try to make the sounds for them) or what happens when you turn the key. This will give experienced mechanics enough information to give you a ballpark estimate of the repair costs.

If you can't get your car to a garage or repair shop without towing it (which can be very expensive), call a few garages and describe the problems you're having. Tell them about your tight budget and ask for a ballpark estimate for the problems you're describing.

Call Around to Compare Your Price

After you know what the problem is, call several garages in your area to find out what they will charge for the same repair. Emphasize that you need to know the total amount and can't afford any surprises. If they won't give you a price, call somewhere else.

If you're going to have it repaired and can't drive it, also call several towing companies to find out how much they'll charge to tow your car to the shop. Keep in mind that your insurance company or travel club may also offer free towing in a limited area. Find this out before you call a tow truck.

Some car repairs are simple enough to do yourself. If you or a friend or family member know anything about cars, consider buying the parts and fixing it yourself. If you have an alternative way to work every day, you can spend a few hours each evening working on your car until it's repaired.

Find Out If the Shop Will Let You Pay over Time

When you find the repair shop that has the best prices and can get the job done quickly, find out whether they'll let you pay over time, say, in three or four payments, without charging interest. They may say no, but it's worth asking.

Develop a New Budget

Using the repair estimates, develop a new budget. Do you have money in savings that you can use? Can you pay the shop a little each month? Can you make the repairs yourself? Can you live without a car and walk, bike, or carpool to work? Can you buy a new-to-you car and still stick with your budget?

FACT

There are several credit cards that help with car expenses, either giving you rebates on gasoline purchases or giving you points that you can use to buy a new or used car, maintain your car (with tune-ups and oil changes, for example), or make needed repairs.

Investigate every possible option, but be realistic in your numbers (see Chapter 4). Whatever route you decide to take—whether that's to make the repair, get another car, or find a way to do without—use your revised budget to begin working toward your financial goals again.

If You Incur Extensive Household Expenses

While you can put off some household repairs, others are critical. If the roof leaks, the sewer drain is clogged, the water isn't running, or you've lost electric power to some of your rooms, you need to get them repaired or replaced. These repairs, however, can be expensive!

The first thing you want to do is try to fix the problem temporarily, so that the repair doesn't blossom into something bigger. Can you, for example, stop the roof's leak by going up into the attic and putting plastic under some of the decking to stop water from coming in? Can you clean out the sewer line with a snake (available from any hardware store)? Have you called the water company to see whether the problem is on its side (that is, in the lines leading up to your water meter)?

Ultimately, however, you're going to have to make one of two choices: Sell the house with the problem or fix the problem. The next two sections discuss these two options.

Sell the House

One way to get out from under large, expensive repairs is to sell your house and move to a smaller one (see Chapter 8 for details on why you would want to do this). The problem, of course, is that either you'll have trouble selling the house to any buyer or you'll have trouble selling it for very much money.

One way to avoid losing too much money is to price the house as though the repair did not have to be made (as if the roof were in great condition, for example), and advertise up front that you'll give back half (or two-thirds, or all) of the amount necessary to make the repair at closing. You won't actually have to come up with that cash out of your savings or other account. Instead, that amount will be subtracted from your equity (the amount of your house that you have paid off) and given to the buyer as a lump sum. You'll get that much less money from selling your house, but you're likely to get more buyers than if you simply price the house lower in the first place. Why? Because many buyers can't afford to make large repairs—they're using all of their cash reserves for the down payment.

ALERT!

Don't ever (ever!) sell your house for less than you owe on the mortgage. If you do this, the lender will immediately demand full payment for the mortgage, and you may not have the money to pay up. Instead, make the repairs.

Here's an example. With a new roof, your house would be worth $90,000. You price it at $84,000 to account for the new roof the buyers will have to get. The buyers are putting 20 percent down and they'd planned on buying a house for $90,000, so they've saved $18,000 for this purpose. If you price the house lower, they'll have to put down only $16,800, so they're able to keep $1,200 of their down-payment money. But $1,200 isn't enough to pay for the roof! Instead, you sell the house for $90,000 but give $6,000 back at closing. They put down their 20 percent ($18,000), but also walk away with a $6,000 check to pay for the roof. And you still get your $84,000 (minus whatever the balance is on your mortgage) and can look for a smaller house.

ESSENTIAL

Many people don't realize that a Realtor's commission may be negotiable. Before signing with a selling agent (also called a listing agent), discuss the commission (usually 3 percent or 3.5 percent to each agent or 6 percent to 7 percent if one agent represents both the buyer and seller). See if your agent will drop down to 3 percent or 2.5 percent for each half of the sale.

If you're thinking of selling your house, keep in mind that many house sales do not require the use of a real estate agent. Because agents get 6 to 7 percent of the selling price of the house, if you don't hire one, you can afford to do a lot of advertising and pay for an attorney or Realtor to draw up the paperwork (which usually costs $500–$1,000), and still come out ahead. Many people use real estate agents because they believe they'll get a higher price for their homes—after all, Realtors get a higher commission if the house sells for more money. But even this may not be true. Most Realtors would rather sell a house cheaply and quickly than price it high and wait for it to sell. If they have to wait an extra three months—and do quite a bit more work showing and advertising the house—to sell it at a higher price, they actually lose money; they'd rather sell it three months earlier for less money.

Keep in mind, however, that if you act as your own agent, you'll have to put up a sign, take out ads in your local paper, and show the house yourself, and you won't have a Realtor to turn to for advice along the way. Use your best judgment. If you take some time to read up on how to sell your own house and think you're up to the task, go for it. If you don't think you'll be successful at selling your own home, shop around for a good Realtor.

Pay for the Repair (but How?)

If you have money in your savings account, even if it was earmarked for something else, you probably want to use it to pay for your home repairs. Short of that, the most logical way to pay for overwhelming household repairs is to refinance your home and cash out some of the equity to pay for the repair. Chapter 10 gives you the scoop on refinancing and tapping your equity.

Even if you don't have much equity in your house (to find your equity, subtract the amount owing on your mortgage from the amount your house is worth), some lenders will still give you cash back, financing your house for up to 120 percent of its value. This can help you pay for your home's repair, but can hurt you in two ways:

- Your monthly payments may soar. (On the other hand, if interest rates are lower than when you bought you house, your monthly payments may stay the same.)
- You may not have any equity in your house if you plan to sell it in a few years.

You never want to finance your home for more than you can sell it for. If your income changes, you might be trapped in your home, unable to sell it and unable to afford the payments.

If Family Medical Bills Overwhelm You

Even if you carry medical insurance, unexpected medical bills can still pile up. Here's why. Suppose your insurance carries a $250 deductible and then pays 80 percent of your medical expenses (your 20 percent is called your co-payment). You are in a car accident that doesn't do any permanent damage to your body, but does result in $15,000 in hospital bills. Of that $15,000, you'll owe $250 for your deductible and $2,950 for your co-payment, for a total of $3,200! Where in the world are you going to come up with that?

Generally, you have only one option: Work out a payment plan with the hospital. (A second option is to pay the bill with your credit card and pay it off aggressively each month, but often the interest rate on credit cards is sky-high.) Some hospitals offer interest-free payments if you pay within three to six months; others charge interest (but usually less than credit card companies charge) no matter how soon you pay.

ALERT!

Never ignore payment notices from a hospital or doctor's office. So many people do this that medical providers are quick to turn to collection agencies and send negative reports to credit-reporting agencies. You may damage your credit rating for years to come.

Most medical providers are willing to work with you to pay off a large balance. They need to know immediately, however, that you'll have trouble paying the balance and want to set up a payment plan.

If you're not sure how much you can pay, revisit your budget. Eliminate any expenses that aren't absolutely required (see Chapters 6 and 7), and see how much you may be able to eke out each month. If this isn't enough, turn to Chapters 8, 9, and 10 for larger-scale ways to cut your expenses. When you've determined how much you can afford to pay each month, approach the medical provider with this amount to see whether it's acceptable. You may have to sign an agreement saying that you'll pay this amount each month—be sure you can pay it before you sign. Remember: Check your budget first. If you're given a monthly amount by the medical provider, don't agree until you've run the numbers on your budget.

If You Become Sick or Disabled— Even Temporarily

If you're in an accident or develop an illness that leaves you disabled even for a short period of time, call your employer immediately. Most employers carry disability insurance on their employees that ranges from 40 to 80 percent of your income, and most can offer you some pay for sick time until that insurance kicks in. Send your employer every bit of information they need to process your claim, including letters from your physician. A call from your doctor to your human resources (HR) representative can also be quite helpful.

Whatever you do, don't get defensive with your employer. Your HR rep should feel as though you're as horrified at your absence as the company is, and that you can't wait to get back to work. Keep in mind that some employees fake illness and injury in order to collect disability pay without working, and you don't want to be labeled as someone who is trying this scam. If the company doesn't believe that you're actually disabled, you could lose more than a few weeks' pay—you could lose your job. You might be able to fight it in court, but that takes money, too. Instead, contact your employer immediately and work with them to resolve your problem.

Even if your company carries disability insurance, however, it may not kick in for some time, and when it does, it won't give you 100 percent of your pay. In this case—or if your company does not carry disability insurance—take the same actions that you would if you lost your job. (See Chapter 12 and the next section in this chapter.)

If You Lose Your Job

If you are laid off from your job, you'll probably feel angry, overwhelmed, and out of control, but this is an important time to stay calm. Not only will you need to keep your wits about you to make the best possible financial decisions, you'll want to watch what you say to coworkers, supervisors, and company representatives. You never know when someone whom you work with now will land at a company you apply to later; you'll want to keep your reputation intact so that you have as many future networking opportunities as possible.

Chapter 12 helps you work through some of the details of unemployment so that you can quickly get back on track with your budget.

If a Friend or Family Member Has a Special Need

Many, many people are in financial trouble because they've given a friend or family member financial assistance that they clearly cannot afford—making a loan that isn't paid back, offering free room and board, buying a car for someone. Don't let this happen to you.

If a friend or family member is in need, you absolutely must help. But, if possible, avoid helping financially unless you can afford to lose that money completely. Always assume that loans won't be paid back or will be defaulted on, expenses associated with free room and board will be completely on your shoulders, and so on. If you can't afford to lose the amount of money that helping your friend will cost, don't help financially. Offer prayers, free babysitting (for a limited period of time), an occasional ride to work, and so on.

Also consider taking your friend to a credit-counseling agency (see Chapter 9) or to a lender to see about getting financial assistance. Don't, however, co-sign any loan that you cannot afford to pay off yourself.

Getting Government Help—There Actually Is a Free Lunch!

If you've cut your expenses to the bone, have tried desperately to find work and couldn't, and still can't scrape together enough money for this week's groceries or this month's rent, you need help. This chapter tells you what free and reduced-cost services are available from the government.

Using Government Food Programs

The Food Stamp Program, WIC, and the National School Lunch Program are the most popular government assistance programs because they allow you to use an electronic benefits transfer card (which resembles a debit card) to purchase core grocery items or to have your children receive meals at school. Without these services, individuals and families in need would go hungry.

The Food Stamp Program

Eligibility for food stamps is surprisingly generous. In fact, many first-year teachers in urban and rural areas (and yes, these are professionals with four-year college degrees) would qualify under the eligibility rules. Here's what those rules look like in general, although they do have several exceptions:

- **Assets.** Up to $2,000 in savings. Note that the value of your car or other vehicle may be treated as an asset, or it may not. Each situation is treated differently, but unless you have a paid-off car that's worth quite a bit, chances are, your car won't be treated as an asset.
- **Income.** Gross (before-tax) income of $1,799 for a family of three, although this amount can vary from state to state and also changes with time.
- **Work.** Every adult, able-bodied member of the family must be working or looking for work.

Food stamps are supposed to be a means of getting through a difficult economic time, but you are allowed to have some money in savings. So as you start to get back on your feet, begin putting a small, but regular, deposit into your savings account.

In addition to these income and savings requirements, you will be asked to register for work (if you're not working already), participate in work-training programs, and accept work if it's offered to you. At that point, your benefits will be reduced or eliminated. To apply for food stamps, call or visit your nearest state food-stamp office.

Food stamps are granted by a formulate that starts with your net monthly household income. More or fewer food stamps may be granted based on whether the household has experienced excessive medical bills or high housing costs, or if they pay a babysitter or child support, and so on. In general, however, an individual receives about $155 in food stamps for the first person in the household, and the scale then slides from $129 for the second person to $117 for the ninth person in the household. Benefits begin the day you apply.

FACT

Although the food stamps program is meant for U.S. citizens, some legally admitted aliens are also eligible. In some states, people applying for food stamps or WIC benefits may also be offered the opportunity to register to vote.

Women, Infants, and Children (WIC)

WIC is a service that offers food distribution (through vouchers that are accepted at many stores and farmer's markets), nutrition counseling, and health-care referrals to pregnant, breastfeeding, and non-breastfeeding new mothers who qualify under income guidelines. The program also offers health-care referrals and food distribution to infants and children of mothers who qualify. The program has been shown to be effective in raising newborn birth weight, lowering infant mortality, and reducing Medicaid costs for pregnant women and their children.

Most areas, even small towns, have a WIC office. Check your local phone book for a location and phone number. Qualifying for WIC is easier than for food stamps. In most states, your household income must not exceed $1,575 per month for one person, and you're allowed about an additional $536 in income per month for each person in your household. The income levels are higher for Alaska and Hawaii because food and housing costs more in those two states. Generally, if you're eligible for food stamps, Medicaid, and other federal-funding programs, you're also eligible for WIC.

The Nutrition Program for the Elderly (NPE)

Like a food-stamp program especially for those age sixty and over, this program provides meals to the elderly, regardless of income. Meals may be offered at a senior citizen's center or may be delivered to homebound residents (frequently called Meals on Wheels). Talk to someone at your local senior citizen's center or call your local Social Security office.

Free Lunch Programs

Through the federal government, kids really can get a free lunch. Like with WIC, most kids who live in households that are eligible for food stamps or Medicaid are automatically eligible for free lunches, reduced-price lunches, free breakfasts, and/or free milk programs. You can contact your child's school to apply.

The National School Lunch Program provides free or reduced-cost lunches, after-school snacks, and nutrition education. The School Breakfast Program provides breakfasts to students who arrive early enough in the morning to require this service. The Summer Food Service Program continues meals and snacks to low-income children during the summer break from school. For children who don't qualify for other meal programs, the Special Milk Program provides milk to children who qualify.

Locating Housing Opportunities

Besides food, housing is often too expensive to afford on your own. The following sections discuss the three basic types of government housing that may be available to you, all of which have stringent qualification standards.

To qualify, you usually have to be paying at least 50 percent of your household income in rent, or you are without a home at this time, or you live in housing that is of exceptionally poor quality (as in, condemned). Even if you were to meet more than one of those three independent tests, waiting lists are very long because the demand exceeds the available apartments. Call the housing authority in your city or state (check the blue pages or government section of your local phone book) and ask how you can apply.

Public Housing

Public housing doesn't have the best reputation in the United States; with few exceptions, it consists of those enormous apartment buildings that are located in some of the most dangerous areas in U.S. cities, and it often has shot-out or otherwise broken windows, malfunctioning plumbing, and other unappealing features. (In smaller towns, they may be better maintained.) If you qualify, however, you generally pay no more than 30 percent of your income in rent.

Section 8 Rental Certificates

Section 8 rental certificates are an interesting contrast to public housing because under this program, you choose where you want to live (from a long list of HUD-approved apartments) and, assuming you qualify, pay no more than 30 percent of your monthly income.

Section 202 Housing

Section 202 housing is for households with at least one very low-income senior citizen who is sixty-two or older. These facilities are not owned by the government; instead, they are private, nonprofit co-operatives. These facilities often provide rooms for disabled seniors and offer meal-delivery services. They also tend to be located in high-quality buildings in safe areas and don't require the use of stairs. Because these facilities are small and often available in rural and suburban areas, seniors who qualify can live close to their relatives.

Applying for Insurance

Not having medical insurance is risky, and yet millions of Americans are without proper insurance. If you go without and have an accident, you could be responsible for thousands of dollars in hospital expenses that you can't afford. Yet, insurance itself is expensive. This section helps you sort out which types of insurance are available from the government.

Understanding Medicare

Medicare is an insurance plan for people age sixty-five and older, for younger Americans who have permanent kidney failure, and for certain disabled citizens. If you qualify and spent ten years of your adult life working in what's called "Medicare-covered employment" (which generally means that you were paid like an employee, not in under-the-table cash payments that were never reported to the federal government), you probably qualify for Part A of the Medicare plan, which covers hospital insurance. If you didn't work enough years, the deductible for this insurance is high—currently from $226 to $410 per month—plus, you pay a deductible of nearly $1,000 per year. But if you worked during much of your adult life, you probably paid for this insurance coverage, so you want to sign up for it.

QUESTION?

Does Medicare cover prescription drugs?
Yes, Medicare does cover some prescription drugs, through Part D. Costs vary widely, as does coverage, deductibles, and copays, depending on which plan you choose under Part D. Visit *www.medicare.gov* for a host of calculators and other explanations that make Part D much easier to understand.

Part B of the Medicare plan does have a premium—currently a little over $90 per month—and it is voluntary. It works exactly like medical insurance (including doctor visits), has a deductible of about $130 per year, and may or may not have copayments. As far as medical insurance goes, paying just over $1,000 per year for coverage that begins after a $130 deductible is phenomenal! Note that, as your income increases, however, the premium for Part B increase as well, but the increases are minor.

For a higher premium, you can also access Medicare Part C, which has better benefits and care.

Looking at Medicaid

Medicaid is a shared federal and state health-insurance program for low-income Americans. Because it's administered by the states, each state determines its own eligibility guidelines, so even if you're eligible for Medicaid in one state, you may not be in another.

Medicaid is very, very difficult to qualify for. Most low-income children, however, are covered in some way—for vaccinations, doctor visits, or hospitalization, for example—as are many low-income pregnant women. Applicants must be medically needy with low income and few, if any, assets or other resources. On the other hand, the "medically needy" standard may make you eligible for Medicaid when you wouldn't otherwise be eligible for state-sponsored low-income services such as welfare.

To get more information on whether you qualify for Medicaid, contact your state social-services and/or human-services agencies. You can find the toll-free number in your phone book.

Getting on Welfare

Welfare used to be nicknamed "the dole." The idea was that if you could get on the welfare doles, you could get away without working a day in your life. The reality was that being on welfare wasn't any fun at all. You filled out mounds of paperwork; got a small weekly or monthly check; were able to just barely make ends meet by using food stamps, government housing, and Medicaid; and never even thought of saving for emergencies, buying a house, or retiring with anything other than a small Social Security check. But you were able to meet the needs of your family in a very basic way.

Welfare has changed quite a bit in the last decade, which means that few resources are available to anyone but the most needy. Welfare, which is administered by the states, is now called Temporary Assistance for Needy Families (TANF), with the emphasis on "temporary." Even if you do qualify, chances are your benefits will last only a short period of time. TANF replaced Aid to Families with Dependent Children (AFDC) and Job Opportunities and Basic Skills Training (JOBS)—the two programs that were known together as welfare.

FACT

Because states administer TANF, whether you'll be eligible is up to the state you live in, and benefits vary greatly, too. States have been mandated by the federal government only to provide assistance, job training, and work opportunities to low-income families; how they choose to do that is up to each state.

Applying for TANF is free, so if your income and resources are sufficiently low and you need temporary assistance (both with your finances and job training) to get you back on your feet, call your local TANF office for information (it may also be listed in the phone book under AFDC, welfare, or JOBS).

Applying for Government Loans and Grants

Besides grants for food, housing, and temporary welfare assistance, state and federal governments offer few opportunities for loans and grants unless you're trying to get help paying for college. See Chapter 18 for information on federal college loan and grant programs for yourself, which may be a long-term way for you to find a way out of your current financial stress.

ESSENTIAL

The federal government offers grants to small businesses, but you'll want to take a seminar or read up on writing grant applications. The process is time-consuming and is practically a full-time job! Still, if you can get a $50,000 grant for your business, the time and energy might be worthwhile.

Loans, in general, aren't a good idea unless the item you're paying for will appreciate (increase) in value with time. This is why home mortgages are considered a good way to spend your money. Although you do pay interest on the mortgage, because the home increases in value, you almost always owe less on the mortgage than the home is worth. (See Chapter 17.)

But if you use loans to pay your rent or buy food, you'll simply put yourself that much deeper into a hole. To get back on solid financial footing, try to use only your own earnings, or the occasional assistance from the government if you absolutely need it, to pay for your expenses in life.

Requesting Bankruptcy Protection

Bankruptcy protection isn't technically a government program, but government courts are responsible for offering you protection from your creditors under bankruptcy laws, so this option is covered in this chapter. You can file two types of cases in bankruptcy court, and they're covered in the two following sections.

Chapter 7

In Chapter 7 bankruptcy, nearly all your debts are wiped out; that is, all unsecured debts (credit card balances, hospital bills, long-distance bills, and so on) are never paid back. Note that unsecured debts to the government, including student loans, taxes, and court-ordered alimony payments, are not wiped out and must continue to be paid back on an agreed-upon schedule.

Secured debt (cars, mortgage on a house, major appliances) is usually sold, and the proceeds pay off the lender. You may, however, get to keep your house (if you keep paying the mortgage), your car (if you keep paying on the loan, should you have one), and some personal property (TV and so on, as long as you don't owe any money on them). However, you generally will not get to retain an expensive house or car; those will have to be sold.

Many people believe that Chapter 7 bankruptcy is a convenient way to run up a bunch of debts and then walk away, scot-free. Perhaps you've even seen ads on TV that encourage you to declare bankruptcy and not have to worry about creditors calling anymore. They tell you that you'll keep your house and maybe even your car, and within a few years, it'll be like it never happened.

Baloney! Chapter 7 bankruptcy is a gut-wrenching heartache that can follow you for at least a decade. Ask yourself this: Why would anyone—especially a creditor who lends money for a living—want to lend you money after you walked away from a pile of unpaid debts in the past? You ate the food, wore the clothes, used the products, and then decided that you didn't want to (or couldn't afford to) pay for them after all. Who would feel compelled to trust you after that? And because you can declare Chapter 7 bankruptcy once every six years, what's going to keep you from doing it again?

Firms that specialize in bankruptcy insist that new creditors won't know about your past, but that's simply not true. A Chapter 7 bankruptcy can stay on your credit report for ten years. And don't forget that potential employers regularly request credit reports before extending an offer to hire you. They figure it tells them something about the sort of person you are—and they may be right! Even the leasing company at the apartment complex you want to move into and the electric company that's setting up electrical service in your name probably won't agree to work with you if they see a bankruptcy on your credit report.

ALERT!

Filing for Chapter 7 bankruptcy protection will cost about $300 in court fees. If you hire a bankruptcy attorney, of course, it'll cost you quite a bit more than that.

Chapter 13

Chapter 13 bankruptcy is so much like credit counseling that it should never be your first choice—credit counseling should be. Like credit counseling (see Chapter 9), you present a plan to the court (including an entire budget that shows that the planned payments are possible) to pay off 100 percent of your debts over as long as five years.

A trustee collects and disperses your payments to creditors, usually charging you an additional 10 percent in the process, an amount that's much higher than what credit counselors charge. You also have to pay about $200 in court fees, and if you use an attorney, you'll have to pay his or her fees. Just about every sort of debt is allowed to be paid off under Chapter 13 bankruptcy, even government loans. Unlike Chapter 7 bankruptcy, with Chapter 13, you usually hold on to your assets.

FACT

According to the Federal Reserve, people filing for bankruptcy typically owe more than one and a half times their annual income in debts (not including their mortgages and cars)! This means that if a family makes $30,000 per year, they owe more than $45,000 in credit card and other high-interest debts.

So why would people choose bankruptcy over credit counseling? Many simply don't know that credit counseling exists, yet chances are you have a nonprofit credit-counseling service right in your city or area. Others believe that bankruptcy is simpler (it isn't) or costs less (it doesn't) than credit counseling. And a few people have had their credit-counseling proposals rejected by creditors, and they see bankruptcy as a last option.

Think of bankruptcy as your last resort; and if you have to choose, file Chapter 13 protection. But always meet with a credit-counseling agency before talking to a bankruptcy lawyer. You'll not only save money, you'll preserve your reputation, too.

Chapter 15

Marriage or Moving In: Budgeting for Two

Ah, love! Ain't it grand? Two people meet, fall in love, and decide to spend the rest of their lives together. It's all about wedding planning, registering, finding a place to cohabitate, and deciding whose sofa is in better shape. All good, right? Well, sure. But keep in mind that the number-one stressor on a relationship is money—either not having enough of it or having widely different ideas about how to make, spend, and save it. So before meeting with your wedding planner, meet with your financial planner. And use the tips and ideas in this chapter to help you both get on the same page.

Don't Let Love Overshadow Finances

Suppose you two are practically perfect for each other: You like the same music; worship at the same church; have similar ideas about how to raise children; and so on. But financially, suppose you're on opposite sides of the map: You believe in working with a budget and saving for a rainy day; he/she figures, if you have money, you spend it, and if you don't, you spend it. You've amassed $18,000 in savings toward the down payment on a house; he/she is $28,000 in debt. You pay cash for your cars and keep them for 200,000 miles; he/she leases a new car every two years. Or vice versa; maybe you're the spender and he/she is the saver.

Regardless, no matter how similar the playlists on your iPods are, you two are not currently a match made in heaven. With your financial goals and ways of living so out of whack, chances are, you're both going to be unhappy.

Before You Move In: Discussing Finances

Sometimes, people spend or save the way they do out of habit. Or, they are not aware that there's any other way to live. Or they've never thought about developing financial goals and working toward them in their everyday financial interactions. If your potential partner is a spender and you're a saver (or vice versa), you don't have to write the relationship off completely.

If either of you is willing to live like the other, there's hope, but if you're both entrenched in your financial ways of living, you're likely going to struggle. To find out, have a serious discussion about finances before formalizing your relationship. In that conversation (or series of conversations), talk about where you see yourself financially in five years, ten years, twenty years, and beyond. Also, make sure you discuss potential financial hotspots by asking the questions listed in **WORKSHEET 15-1.**

WORKSHEET 15-1
Financial Hotspots for Couples

How much income do you make?

How many assets do you have, and how much debt do you have?

As a general rule, how much money are you comfortable keeping in savings?

What percentage of your income do you like to contribute or otherwise give away?

How would you respond if a friend or family member asks to borrow money?

Would you rather rent or buy a place to live? If rent, for how long?

What's the highest monthly mortgage payment you'd be comfortable with?

Do you eventually see yourself being mortgage-free? If so, in how many years?

How do you feel about having credit card or store charge-card debt?

Do you pay off your credit cards or store-charge cards every month?

Do you prefer to lease a new car, buy a car on credit, or save to pay cash for a car?

How important is it to you to be able to eat out one or more nights per week, get take-out regularly, and stop by the coffee shop every morning?

How often do you shop for new clothes or buy new toys (electronics, golf clubs, etc.)? Do you pay cash for these items?

Do you ever want to join a country club or athletic club?

What sort of vacations do you see yourself taking? What sort of places would you like to go? At what category of hotel would you stay?

Have you already started saving for retirement? At what age do you plan to retire?

Regarding children, how do you feel about giving an allowance versus giving them money when they want/need it?

Will you buy your children cars when they turn sixteen? Will you pay for their gas, insurance, and maintenance?

Will you pay for your children's college costs? If so, all or a portion?

Will you pay for a child's wedding? If so, all or a portion?

How do you anticipate caring for your aging parents, if they need assistance? Will we pay for their care? Will they live with us?

For help in dealing with differences in financial goals, check out the "Finding Compromise in Different Approaches to Finances" section later in this chapter. For further steps in merging your financial goals, visit the "Creating a Two-Person Budget" section at the end of this chapter.

Deciding Where to Live

Ideally, couples newly married or moving in together will rent for a year rather than buy a house, especially if either is new to the area. Renting for your first year gives you time to determine how much room the two of you need to live comfortably, in which area of town you both wish to live, and how much home you can afford. Renting also gives you time to look at houses together, which will likely spark discussions about what each is looking for in a home. Through these discussions, you will eventually find a home that fits both of you.

FACT

The online payment company PayPal surveyed over 3,000 people and found that, for couples between ages eighteen and forty, 82 percent said money was the number-one issue in their relationship.

Many couples—especially older couples and those marrying for the second time—will move into the house of one or the other person. If nothing else makes financial sense, then make this move. But if selling one or both existing houses and buying a new one together also makes financial sense, take that route instead. Why? Because the partner who moves into the other's house will likely always feel like a guest there, and no one should feel like a guest in his or her own home. If you find that you must take this step, make the house as much of a blank slate as possible: Move all the furniture out of the house; repaint and redecorate as much as your budget can afford; and then merge the possessions of both parties and, perhaps, purchase a few key furnishings together.

Choosing Between Single and Joint Accounts

One of the first decisions you'll have to make when you and your significant other move in together is how to merge your finances. You have two main options:

- Open a joint checking account, deposit both your paychecks into that account, and jointly pay all bills out of that account. This is the option that most married couples choose, because it simplifies the question of "How much money do we have?" Most people who have a joint checking account also have joint everything else: Credit cards; retirement accounts; savings accounts; and so on. If you choose this option, however, be sure to designate one person as the official bill payer in the family. Also, you need to find a way to keep track of the amounts that are debited from the account (through debit cards, checks, and Internet payments) each day or week.

- Keep separate accounts, as they were before you moved in together. Each person's paycheck goes into his or her account, and the bills are divided up, with each paying a share of the bills. This is the option most unmarried couples choose. It offers the most autonomy and independence, but it can create resentment, especially if one person makes significantly more than the other, and thus has substantially more spending money. To combat this problem, some couples divide the bills according to income, so that if one person makes 40 percent more than the other, he or she also pays 40 percent more of the bills than the other, thus leaving both with similar cash for spending.

ESSENTIAL

Prenuptial agreements may seem like the least romantic idea you've ever heard, but a recent Harvard University study found that prenups usually aren't primarily about money. Instead, they detail how the couple plans to raise children, under what grounds the couple can divorce, and so on. Prenups usually mean that the couple has spent significant time talking about how they see the marriage working, and that can only be good.

Finding Compromise in Different Approaches to Finances

If you find (perhaps after completing **WORKSHEET 15-1**) that you and your significant other have significantly different approaches to finances, you don't necessarily have to call it quits. But before you take the next step, have a long, hard, honest talk about finances.

ALERT!

Given how important money is in relationships, if you can't agree on that, it really doesn't matter how good everything else is. Take any substantial money disagreements very seriously before getting married!

Discuss ways in which you can compromise. For example, suppose a couple has radically different views about money. They both make good income, but she has spent most of college in debt, and he had his college paid for. She's adamant about getting out of debt, and then saving for retirement, buying a house, and planning for children. She doesn't enjoy golf, and he's an avid golfer who can either play on the public course for about $3,000 per year or join a country club for $10,000 per year. He's a spender who doesn't think much about money, so he really wants the country-club option; she thinks the country club is a waste of money that moves them away from more important financial goals.

At this point, they appear to have three options: 1) Go with the public course; 2) join the country club; or 3) break up. But perhaps there's a compromise to be had. For every dollar above the public-course fee that he spends (so, $7,000 per year), the couple can also put a dollar toward her student loan until it's paid off, and then toward savings and a retirement account after the loan is paid off. That way, he gets to join the country club, but they also meet her financial goals. If they can't afford to do both, at least her financial goals are put on the same footing as his golfing goals.

Creating a Two-Person Budget

In order to create a two-person budget, you and your significant other should sit down together and go through Chapters 1 through 4. Come up with financial goals (both individual ones and joint ones), track your individual spending, and establish a budget that works for both of you. Use **WORKSHEET 15-2** for your final data, but be sure to go through the steps in Chapters 1 through 4 so that the budget you establish represents your shared vision of your financial future.

WORKSHEET 15-2
Two-Person Budget

Monthly Expense	Amount
Groceries and household items	$
Day care	$
Contributions	$
Savings	$
Rent on furniture or appliances	$
Entertainment/babysitting	$
Eating out	$
Rent or mortgage	$
Car payment or lease	$
Electric bill (average)	$
Gas bill (average)	$
Water bill	$
Sewer bill	$
Trash pick-up bill	$
Cable/DSL/satellite bill	$
Telephone bill	$
Cell-phone bill	$
Bank charges	$

WORKSHEET 15-2

Two-Person Budget (*continued*)

Monthly Expense	Amount
Haircuts/manicures/pedicures	$
Home equity loan	$
Other loan	$
Credit card or store-charge bill	$
Credit card or store-charge bill	$
Credit card or store-charge bill	$
Credit card or store-charge bill	$
Credit card or store-charge bill	$
Credit card or store-charge bill	$
Credit card or store-charge bill	$
Child support or alimony	$
Car maintenance	$
House maintenance	$
Auto insurance	$
Property taxes	$
Gifts	$
Events to attend	$
Clothing and shoes	$
Home insurance	$
Vehicle registration	$
Vacation	$
Club membership	$
Other:	$
Other:	$
TOTAL:	$

Chapter 16

Changing Your Budget for a New Baby

Having a new baby is a wonderful event in your life, but also a stressful one. Babies bring multitudes of blessings and multitudes of expenses. This chapter helps you budget for the expenses of having a baby, both now and when that baby is ready for college!

Making Time to Think about Your Future

When you find out that you're pregnant, you'll be amazed, thrilled, stressed, and overwhelmed, maybe even in that order. A baby is a remarkable addition to a household, and that thought will sustain you for some time. But before long, you may begin to sweat when you think about the medical costs of having a baby, and then the diapers, clothing, bigger house, furniture for the nursery, toys, books, stroller, car seat, and then, eventually, a car and college tuition!

Before you panic, set aside time to plan your finances around your new baby. If possible, do your planning early in the pregnancy so that you're aware of all the potential expenses as you go along and aren't stressed for nine long months.

ESSENTIAL

Any time you begin to panic, think of your greatest fear in the situation: You'll spend so much money on your baby that you'll be homeless; or you'll have to work so much to pay the bills that you'll make a terrible parent. Whatever the fear, think it through, and then, if possible, get a good laugh from it. You're too far along the budgeting track to let something like that happen!

Sit down with this chapter and work your way through it step by step. If you don't know the price for a particular product or service, find out, and then meet back here to complete this chapter.

Estimating Expenses for Your New Baby

Your first step in calmly revising your budget to include your new little room-mate is to estimate your new baby expenses. You do this by interviewing people, reading, visiting stores, calling about services, and so on. The following sections detail the information you're looking for.

Interview Other New Parents

Talk to everyone you know who has had a baby recently, and begin to find out what expenses they incurred. Don't be surprised if the talk is mostly negative—people may tell you that they've practically gone broke because of a new baby—and try not to let it affect you. Their finances are not your finances, and you may be able to make very different decisions than they made. Brace yourself, though, for lots of advice on what to buy and what not to buy, what to do and what not to do. Even if it's annoying, you can gather great information about what expenses were unexpected, what were the good investments, and so on. Keep good notes, thank them for their time, use their information to estimate your expenses, and then proceed to do whatever is best for your finances.

Read One Good Baby Book

Baby books can answer all the questions you have, even ones you didn't know to ask! For example, how long do babies breastfeed? After they start eating baby food, how much will they eat? How many diapers do babies go through in a day? What are the essential supplies that babies need, and which are extras that you may be able to do without? How often do they have to visit the doctor? What symptoms warn you that an extra doctor visit is required? Which vaccines do babies need to get? How fast do babies grow? Do they wear shoes? When do they need hearing and eye exams? What about dental visits? Do babies need their own books? How many and which books do they need?

Mine your local library for baby books before visiting a bookstore. While you may eventually decide to buy a baby book as a reference to have around the house, reading those at the library first can keep you from spending money on duds.

If you haven't been around children very much, a good book on babies can answer even your most basic questions. And if you're a bit of a baby expert, most baby books serve as good reminders of the information you already know; plus they usually have little nuggets of great information that you've never heard before.

Visit Stores, Including Online Shops

One of the easiest ways to begin thinking of what expenses a baby may create is to visit a store—brick and mortars or online—and see what products are offered for babies. Keep in mind that you don't have to buy the vast majority of this stuff, just like adults don't need half of the products that are marketed for them, but stores are a good place to start. Write down everything you see, from baby diapers and bottles to bassinettes and cribs.

ESSENTIAL

Don't forget that you may have a baby shower thrown in your honor, which will allow you to receive some of the items you need as presents. It's likely you won't have to buy every item on your list!

If the store you're visiting offers a baby-shower registry service, see if you can get the list they ask prospective parents to fill out. You don't necessarily have to register (some people think it's a great tool; others feel it's gratuitous), but the list itself will help you identify what items other people buy for their babies.

Don't forget to visit grocery stores, too, to determine the cost of baby food. Breastfeeding is both the healthiest and most economical way to feed your child for the first year or so, but after that, you'll need to start buying a variety of baby foods. Determine whether you want to buy organic or non-organic baby food, and then take notes about how much they cost. You can also make your own baby food with only a few common kitchen tools and fresh fruits and vegetables. If you're interested, check out books on the subject from your local bookstore or library.

Take Stock of What You Already Own

You may already own quite a bit of furniture that can be used in a baby's room. If you have an armoire; a dresser or chest of drawers; or an upholstered chair, small sofa, or rocker in any other room of your house, consider moving it into the nursery for a year or so. Even furniture that doesn't look great can be painted in bright or pastel colors to look attractive. Just be sure that the furniture is sturdy and sliver-free so that it won't end up hurting your child.

FACT

A great place to get inexpensive baby supplies is at tag sales (also called yard sales and garage sales). Look for those that advertise baby clothes, toys, furniture, and so on. You may be able to pick up onesies (these are one-piece outfits that babies wear) for a quarter—several dollars less than you would pay at even the cheapest store.

Call Around to Price Services

If you're thinking of using a diaper service, day-care service, or babysitter, call several in your area and compare their prices and levels of service. It's especially important to interview day-care providers and babysitters to make sure their philosophy on childrearing is the same as yours.

Note that although diaper service is going out of fashion in favor of disposable diapers, diaper services can save you money. Instead of continuously buying and throwing-away diapers, you essentially rent them from a diaper service. They drop off clean diapers and pick up dirty ones, and when you no longer need them, you stop the service. The upside is that you don't have to pay the high cost of disposables; the downside is that some babies have reactions to the strong chemicals used to clean the dirty diapers. But some babies react to disposable diapers, too.

Call Your Medical-Insurance Company

If you don't have a schedule of services for your medical insurance policy, call your representative to find out how much the pregnancy, natural-childbirth classes, delivery, and baby visits are going to cost (your deductible plus the copay). Also, find out whether your premiums will rise because of the extra person who will now be on your policy.

ALERT!

If you aren't yet ready for your employer to know you're pregnant, wait to call your medical insurance company until you've told them. You don't want your employer to discover your news from a third party.

If you don't currently have medical insurance, call your doctor and local hospital to get an estimate on how much having a baby and keeping him or her healthy is going to cost. If you don't have the cash, also find out whether they have a payment plan. And don't rule out the possibility of using a midwife for the delivery. Unless your pregnancy is high risk, using a midwife can be an effective way to reduce your costs. You can often deliver the child in your own home, saving thousands of dollars in hospital fees. Keep in mind, however, that you won't have the medical resources of the hospital on call. If something goes wrong during a home delivery, both the baby's and the mother's health can be at risk.

If You're Thinking of Moving, Look at Housing Prices

Many people believe that a new baby has to result in a new house, and that may be so if you're living in a one-bedroom house with no bathtub. But babies are very small, at least for a while, and you may be able to fit your baby into even a small house for a year or two before moving. If your house has two or more bedrooms, you may not need to move for several years, if at all. If you do decide to move, take a look at housing prices in the area first, so that you can use this information to create your baby-friendly budget. Using an online mortgage calculator (see Appendix B), determine how much your monthly mortgage payments will rise.

If you can afford it, getting a fifteen-year mortgage when your baby is born is a great way to pay for college: You'll have three years of "mortgage payments" (that actually go into your savings account) before you have to write the first tuition check. See Chapter 17 for more information.

Putting Your Figures Together in One Worksheet

After gathering all the information you can find on how much your new baby may cost you, put it together in **WORKSHEET 16-1.** List every baby expense you can think of, along with the monthly cost. Then take a careful look at the list and determine which items you really need and which you can reduce or do without.

WORKSHEET 16-1
Baby Expenses

Expense	Monthly Costs
	$
	$
	$
	$
	$
	$
	$
	$
	$
	$
	$
	$
TOTAL:	$

Creating a Nine-Month Savings Budget

Although the long gestation period for human babies results in a lot of discomfort for the mother, there is one silver lining: You get nine months to save up for the added expense a baby brings. Think of the time until your baby is born as your best chance to save. Cut back on every possible expense between now and then (see Chapters 5 through 8 for more ideas) and save every penny you can.

Having money in savings when your baby is born can help in a variety of ways: You can pay for medical expenses; use it to live on should you or your spouse decide not to return to work; pay for a day-care provider; use it as a cushion against unexpected repairs on your house or car; and so on. Use **WORKSHEET 16-2** to help you determine how much you can save.

WORKSHEET 16-2
A Nine-Month Savings Budget

Monthly Expense	Amount	Ways to Reduce/Eliminate	New Amount
Savings for the baby	$	N/A	$
Groceries and household items	$		$
Contributions	$		$
Rent on furniture or appliances	$		$
Entertainment/babysitting	$		$
Eating out	$		$
Rent or mortgage	$		$
Car payment or lease	$		$
Electric bill (average)	$		$
Gas bill (average)	$		$
Water bill	$		$
Sewer bill	$		$
Trash pick-up bill	$		$
Cable/DSL/satellite bill	$		$
Telephone bill	$		$

WORKSHEET 16-2

A Nine-Month Savings Budget (*continued*)

Monthly Expense	Amount	Ways to Reduce/Eliminate	New Amount
Cell-phone bill	$		$
Bank charges	$		$
Haircuts/manicures/pedicures	$		$
Home equity loan	$		$
Other loan	$		$
Credit card or store-charge bill	$		$
Credit card or store-charge bill	$		$
Credit card or store-charge bill	$		$
Credit card or store-charge bill	$		$
Credit card or store-charge bill	$		$
Credit card or store-charge bill	$		$
Child support or alimony	$		$
Car maintenance	$		$
House maintenance	$		$
Auto insurance	$		$
Property taxes	$		$
Gifts	$		$
Events to attend	$		$
Clothing and shoes	$		$
Home insurance	$		$
Vehicle registration	$		$
Vacation	$		$
Club membership	$		$
	$		$
TOTAL:	$		$

Choosing a Daytime Care Provider

Before your baby is born, you'll want to decide who is going to care for this baby throughout the workday. If you currently work nine or ten hours per day, someone has to be watching the baby during that time. The following sections review your child-care options, which are presented in no particular order.

Day-Care Center

Day-care centers have been growing steadily in popularity for the last twenty years or so. In a day-care center, which ranges in cost from a low of about $150 per week to a high of about $500 per week, your child will be one of many children his or her age. The setting is usually very much like a school, except, perhaps, brighter and a bit cozier. Children are usually fed a couple of snacks and a lunch; they may or may not play outside very much. Some day-care centers accept newborns, while others take only children who are six months of age or older.

To find out which centers are the best in your area, ask friends, family, neighbors, and coworkers for recommendations. Then visit the center, more than once, if possible. Although you'll want to arrange a visit your first time, feel free to drop in unannounced the next time. You have every right to see how children at the center are treated all the time, not just when a parent is expected.

ALERT!

If you are breastfeeding, and you plan to put a newborn in day care, find out from your physician how to use a breast pump, so that your baby can continue to use breast milk as his or her source of food. While this is not the most convenient way to feed your baby, it is the cheapest!

If you're lucky enough to have an on-site day-care center at work, you'll be able to spend your work breaks and lunch with your child, and you may even pay a discounted fee for child care. On-site day-care centers are rare, so if you have one, consider it one of your best options. If you don't, consider looking for a new job that does include this benefit. See Chapter 8 for more information.

Daytime Babysitter

Another option is to use a daytime babysitter, either in your own home or in the home of the babysitter. (Live-in nannies, who work for room, board, and a small salary, fall under this category.) Usually, daytime babysitters care for only a few children of varying ages at one time—their own and one or two others. Even the most caring babysitter can't watch, care for, and stimulate more children than that at one time. Some daytime babysitters are able to take on newborns; others choose not to. Babysitters usually, but not always, prefer to stay in their own homes during the day. They may ask you to provide lunch and snacks, or they may provide them for you (charging more, of course, for that service). Prices range from a low of $120 a week to a high of several hundred per week. Live-in nannies can be the most expensive because they require their own bedrooms and baths, plus food and a small salary.

Personal recommendations from family, friends, neighbors, and coworkers is the best way to locate a daytime babysitter.

Grandparents

Having one of your child's grandparents care for him or her is exactly like using a daytime babysitter, except that grandparents usually charge far less. In fact, some grandparents who are retired are eager to spend as much time as possible with their grandchildren and don't charge a penny for the service. While this is often the case, don't expect it from your own parents. If a grandparent has offered to care for your child during the day, discuss fees early in the conversation.

You or Your Spouse

The advantage of having others care for your child is that you can continue working as you have in the past. The disadvantages are threefold:

- People with other values, disciplinary tactics, energy levels, and education levels are caring for your child.
- You get to spend far less time—and often the times when you're most fatigued—with your child.
- Paying for a child-care provider often costs more than your income brings in after taxes, commuting costs, dry cleaning, and so on are subtracted.

As a result, many people choose to care for their own children. You can do this in a variety of ways:

- Work a different shift than your spouse does (either full time or part time), and each care for your child while the other works.
- Both of you work part time (for example, one works mornings and the other works afternoons), and each care for your child while the other works.
- One works full time and the other cares for your child during the workday.

If you both decide to work, but on different shifts, you won't experience any reduction in pay, which is good. The downside, however, is that you and your spouse will rarely see each other, and you didn't get married so that you could leave each other notes on the kitchen counter. If you choose this option, it should be extremely temporary. For example, until you can save enough for one of you to stay home full time or until the baby is old enough to be accepted at a day-care facility.

Living on One Income

If you or your spouse plans to care for your child, you'll have to decide which one is best equipped to do this. Nowhere is it written that women are better at caring for their children full time than men are, so if the child's father is willing and able to leave his job to care for the baby, that may well be your best option.

Many people decide who will stay home solely on finances: The person with the best-paying job keeps working, while the other stays home. Don't forget, however, to factor in medical insurance (if both have it, whose is cheaper and better?) and the commute. **WORKSHEET 16-3** can help you work through the numbers.

Whenever possible, don't base this decision entirely on finances. One parent may simply be better suited to or more interested in providing child care and will, therefore, be better at it. Factor this into your equation, too.

WORKSHEET 16-3

Are Two Incomes Better Than One?

Income	Working	Staying Home
Take-home pay	$	$
Lost retirement contribution	$	$
Total Income:	$	$
Expense	**Working**	**Staying Home**
Outside child-care costs	$	$
Increased medical-insurance costs	$	$
Decrease in car expenses	$	$
Decrease in lunches out	$	$
Decrease in dry-cleaning	$	$
Increase in heating and electricity	$	$
Total Expenses:	$	$

Creating a Budget for Your New Family

Now that you have an idea of the expenses your new baby will bring, along with the potential loss of income that caring for your child can entail, you can create a new, baby-friendly budget. Use **WORKSHEET 16-4** (and the instructions for developing and refining a budget in Chapter 4) to determine how you're going to afford your new baby.

WORKSHEET 16-4
New-Baby Budget

Monthly Expense	Amount	Ways to Reduce/Eliminate	New Amount
Groceries and household items	$		$
Contributions	$		$
Savings	$		$
Rent on furniture or appliances	$		$
Entertainment/babysitting	$		$
Eating out	$		$
Rent or mortgage	$		$
Car payment or lease	$		$
Electric bill (average)	$		$
Gas bill (average)	$		$
Water bill	$		$
Sewer bill	$		$
Trash pick-up bill	$		$
Cable/DSL/satellite bill	$		$
Telephone bill	$		$
Cell phone bill	$		$
Bank charges	$		$
Haircuts/manicures/pedicures	$		$
Home equity loan	$		$
Other loan	$		$
Credit card or store-charge bill	$		$
Credit card or store-charge bill	$		$
Credit card or store-charge bill	$		$
Credit card or store-charge bill	$		$
Credit card or store-charge bill	$		$

WORKSHEET 16-4
New-Baby Budget (*continued*)

Monthly Expense	Amount	Ways to Reduce/Eliminate	New Amount
Credit card or store-charge bill	$		$
Child support or alimony	$		$
Car maintenance	$		$
House maintenance	$		$
Auto insurance	$		$
Property taxes	$		$
Gifts	$		$
Events to attend	$		$
Clothing and shoes	$		$
Home insurance	$		$
Vehicle registration	$		$
Vacation	$		$
Club membership	$		$
Other:	$		$
Other:	$		$
TOTAL:	$		$

Chapter 17

Changing Your Budget to Include a New House

Deciding to buy your first house or to leave your existing home for a different one is exciting, but figuring out how to save for a down payment and afford the monthly mortgage payments isn't always easy. This chapter helps you figure out the details.

Figuring Out the Financing Details

Most people have to finance a house in order to buy it. Of course, some shrewd budgeters—especially those who are nearing retirement—have a paid-off house, so when they go to sell it, they pocket the money and can pay cash for the next one.

Ultimately, most people want to know how much the monthly payment will be, and that's a function of the length of mortgage you choose (fifteen years versus thirty years, for example), your down payment, and the prevailing interest rate. To find out how much of a monthly payment you'll end up owing, visit SmartMoney's mortgage calculator at *www.smartmoney.com*. Click on the Personal Finance tab, then scroll down to the Real Estate section on the left-hand side of the screen and click on The Mortgage Calculator. There you'll find out everything from how much your monthly payment will be to how much of a difference the mortgage length, down payment, and interest rate make.

Don't forget to add on the cost of PMI (private mortgage insurance) and escrow to the monthly bill. Although not everyone has to pay these costs (they're discussed in "Recognizing Other Costs of Low-Down-Payment Mortgages" later in this chapter), if you do, they will be added to your monthly payment amount.

Choosing Your Mortgage Length

In order to know how much you'll need to save to buy a house, you first need to make some basic mortgage decisions. This section (as well as the next two) helps you understand some of the financial decisions surrounding buying your house.

Your equity (the value of your home minus the amount of your mortgage) increases as you pay off your mortgage and as your house increases in value. If you pay more than the amount due each month, you'll increase your equity much faster than if you pay only the minimum amount due.

Although choosing your mortgage length may seem like a simple, straightforward decision, it's actually one that will have a tremendous impact on your financial security over the next several decades of your life.

Thirty-Year Versus Fifteen-Year Mortgages

The majority of Americans getting a new mortgage on a home opt for a thirty-year loan without even considering other options. A thirty-year loan is what all your friends, family, and neighbors have probably signed up for, and it does make the monthly payment much more affordable than a fifteen-year mortgage.

So what's the problem with getting a thirty-year mortgage? Although the following is a general statement that doesn't hold true for every mortgage amount and every interest rate, here's a simple rule of thumb: With a thirty-year loan, you'll end up paying a little less than one and a half times the mortgage amount in interest over the life of the loan. This means that if you buy a $100,000 house, you'll pay nearly $140,000 in addition to the price of the home, just for the privilege of stringing the payments out over thirty years. Now think about what you could do with $140,000! That would make a pretty good retirement nest egg, wouldn't it? Whatever you'd like to spend $140,000 on, spending it on virtually nothing doesn't seem like a very good idea, yet that's what you do when you get a thirty-year loan.

Proponents of mortgages will tell you that because you can deduct the mortgage interest on Schedule A of your federal income taxes, spending all that money on mortgage interest is a good idea, but the numbers don't bear that out. Suppose you pay $6,400 per year in interest on your mortgage, and you're in a 22-percent tax bracket. This means you can deduct $1,408 from your taxes this year. Over the life of a thirty-year loan, that's $42,240 in taxes you don't have to pay and can put into your retirement, business, or Corvette fund. But if you pay $140,000 in interest over those thirty years, you're still out nearly $100,000 in interest!

A better idea is to reduce the life of your loan to fifteen years, or less. If you pay off that same house in fifteen years, you'll pay only about $60,000 in interest and get about $10,500 in tax savings. This means that by paying off your mortgage fifteen years early (even if you take the tax deductions), you've earned yourself a $50,000 gift.

Generally, you'll find two lengths of mortgages: Fifteen years or thirty years. Occasionally, you might be able to get a mortgage for a length other than fifteen or thirty years, but few lenders offer them. If your goal is to pay off your house in full as soon as possible, and if you have a large down payment, ask about a five- or ten-year mortgage. They're rare and may require some additional costs and paperwork, but locking in to a short mortgage will force you to pay it off quickly.

Paying Any Mortgage Off Early

Another way to shorten your mortgage, however, is to simply pay more than the required amount each month. Here's another simple rule: If you make one extra payment per year (or if you divide the amount of one payment by twelve months and add that to each month's payment), you'll cut about seven years off the life of your thirty-year loan.

QUESTION?

How do I pay off my mortgage in ten years?
To pay off your house in ten years, use a mortgage calculator (or ask your lender) to figure out how much extra you'll need to pay each month. Pay that extra amount each month, and in ten years, the mortgage will be paid off.

Although you may want to lock in the shortest possible mortgage length to take advantage of the lower interest rate that goes along with it, going with a longer mortgage length may give you more flexibility in your finances. For example, you can get the great rate associated with a fifteen-year loan, but plan to pay it off in ten years. Of course, if you're not disciplined enough to pay the extra, lock in that higher payment.

Deciding on a Down Payment

Just one or two generations ago, you couldn't buy a house without a 20-percent down payment. That meant that many people were effectively locked out of ever owning a home. So the last twenty years have seen major changes in how Americans buy homes. You can now buy a home with 10-, 3-, 1-, or even 0-percent down.

While these smaller down payments have allowed more people than ever to afford home ownership, they (in combination with home equity lines of credit and second mortgages) have made the concept of having a lot of equity in your house—and eventually paying it off—seem old-fashioned.

Here's the thing, though: Not only is a big down payment not old-fashioned, it actually makes great financial sense. You know from the preceding section that paying off your loan in fifteen years instead of thirty saves you a bundle of money. In the same way, the larger you can make your down payment, the more you're going to save on interest charges over the life of your loan. This is because you finance the amount of house that you don't own, and you own all of your down payment. So, if you put $40,000 down on a $200,000 house, you incur finance charges only on your $160,000 mortgage, but if you put zero down, you'll pay much more in interest rates over the life of the loan because you'll incur finance charges on $200,000.

Seeing the Big Picture, Not Just the Monthly Payment

Many people think only in terms of monthly payment, and the truth is, each $1,000 you put down on your house lowers your payment by only a few dollars a month. To really expand your financial opportunities, though, and have lots of options for how you live your life, try seeing beyond the monthly payments to the loan amount itself. If you can put 20-percent down on a house and pay it off in ten years by making very aggressive payments each month, in ten years you'll have way more income than you'll know what to do with! The point is, you'll have options that simply don't exist if you lock in to a 3-percent down, thirty-year mortgage.

A Closer Look at Low Down-Payment Mortgages

With a low down-payment mortgage, you'll incur a few other costs, too. When you put less than 20-percent down on a house, your lender will collect a portion of your homeowner's insurance and property taxes every month and hold it in escrow (a fancy name for a savings account), and then pay your taxes and insurance directly. This "convenience" costs you plenty, however, because the bank—not you—earns interest on that escrow account, sometimes as much as a few hundred dollars a year! If you make a larger down payment, or as you build-up equity in your house, you can eliminate that escrow account.

A common theory is that instead of putting a big down payment into your house, you should put down as little as possible and invest that money instead. Look at this option carefully, though. Most investments don't regularly make more than 6 percent to 8 percent a year, which is what many mortgages charge. Chances are, you'll come out exactly even.

In addition, when you put less than 20-percent down, the lender will probably charge you PMI (private mortgage insurance), which insures the lender against the potential of your defaulting on the mortgage. But what most people don't know is that as you build up equity in your house, you can get your PMI cancelled. Ask your lender about its PMI rules.

Reviewing Your Interest-Rate Options

Whether to go with a fixed- or variable-interest loan is an easier question than how long to make your mortgage or how large to make your down payment.

Here's the rule: If interest rates are relatively low, get a fixed-rate loan, which means that the interest rate will stay the same throughout the life of your loan. If interest rates are high, however, get a variable-rate loan that changes daily, weekly, or monthly—it's sure to come down when interest rates drop again.

Most variable-rate loans are for just five years or so. The idea is that you'll refinance at the end of that time (or sooner) and lock into a lower, fixed-interest rate. If interest rates are not low when you buy a house, plan to refinance when they drop—and work the costs associated with refinancing (called closing costs, which are discussed in "Understanding Closing

Expenses" near the end of this chapter) into your budgeted savings. See Chapter 10 for more on mortgage refinancing.

Shopping for Your New Home

Shopping for a new home can be stressful, but it can also be great fun. The following sections can help you understand some of the ins and outs of shopping for your new home. And don't forget to visit the government's Ginnie Mae Web site at *www.ginniemae.gov*. There you'll find a Homeownership Information Center that can give you plenty of detail about home ownership.

The house you buy should be relatively soundproof; have a friend walk upstairs while you're downstairs and talk out loud from an adjoining room with the doors shut. Also look for heavy doors, insulated windows, and quality flooring. Finally, look for a house that, in the last five years, has received a new roof, furnace, and windows.

Getting Preapproved

Preapproval means that you're definitely going to qualify for a mortgage if you buy a house in a particular price range. Sellers like preapproved buyers because the sellers have the assurance that if they accept a preapproved buyer's bid, the deal will very likely go through. Accepting a bid from a buyer who isn't preapproved doesn't carry this same guarantee.

Note that preapproval is different from prequalification. Prequalification isn't worth the paper it's printed on—it just means that the lender is eager to find out more about you and decide whether you're a worthy credit risk.

Working Alone or with a Realtor

If you're a first-time home buyer, you probably want to use a Realtor, who will show you a variety of homes in your price range. Working with a

Realtor isn't mandatory, of course, and some seasoned home buyers often don't use them unless they're trying to buy a house in a different city or in a very short time frame.

Keep an eye on interest rates before deciding to move. The Internet can help you track interest rates over the last few months, and that information can help you decide what a good rate is and whether to lock in now or wait.

Making an Offer

When you find the home of your dreams, you need to make an offer on the house. In some areas where housing is in great demand and prices are exorbitantly high, sellers won't even consider an offer that isn't at or above the asking price (that's the price advertised). But in many areas, offering 5 to 10 percent less than the asking price is standard practice. An experienced Realtor can shed some light on which type of offer you should make.

Whatever you do, don't buy a poorly built house in a bad location to save money. If you choose a bad location, you're likely to have a hard time reselling the house in the future. If you buy a house that's in need of substantial repair or was made with cheap components, you'll end up being overloaded with repairs and maintenance.

Even if you submit an offer at or above the asking price, it's still not guaranteed to be accepted. Sellers can pretty much do whatever they want with offers—except discriminate against you on the basis of ethnicity, gender, or religion.

When you write up an offer, be sure to make the sale of the house contingent on the following:

- Selling your existing house (so you're not stuck with two houses)
- A clean inspection (or that defects found during an inspection will be repaired by the seller)
- A clear title (that no one else actually owns the house)
- Obtaining financing (so that you're not legally obligated to buy the house by paying cash for it)
- Including everything you list in the offer (Do you expect the sellers to leave the appliances, curtains, and wooden flower pots on the porch?)

Selling Your Existing Home

If you own a home already, you'll probably want to sell it before moving into your new home. Selling a house is a big job, so don't plan on spending any time on your hobbies for a while!

Working Alone or with a Realtor

The first decision you have to make is whether you want to sell it yourself or use a Realtor. Unlike when you're buying a house, this decision is about more than convenience, it's about money. Realtors charge the seller, not the buyer, for their services. If a Realtor lists your house and brings you a buyer for it, that agent gets a 6- or 7-percent commission. If, on the other hand, a Realtor lists your house and another agent brings a buyer for it, the two agents split the 6- or 7-percent commission between them.

This can end up being a lot of money. Some real-estate agents earn every penny of that commission, and you can't figure out how you ever lived without them. But others just don't do three-, four-, or ten-thousand-dollars worth of work, and your house languishes.

If you've never sold a house before, you may want to use a Realtor. But if you're experienced at buying and selling houses and/or you're confident in your ability to market your own house successfully, go it alone. You'll find blank real-estate conveyance forms at your local library, and you'll probably pay $500 or $1,000 (splitting this fee with the buyer) to a local lawyer to draw up the paperwork.

Getting It Ready to Sell

If you've been living in your house the way most people do, your house probably isn't ready to sell. Houses that are up for sale have usually had many small repairs made, windows and siding cleaned, mailbox replaced, fences and interior walls spruced up and painted, flowerbeds weeded and new ones planted, and so on. Many real-estate professionals also recommend replacing every light bulb in your house with a new one, and then turning on all the lights in your house whenever a potential buyer tours it. Some people also bake bread every time someone is coming to see a house; the homey smell makes people think they want to live there forever!

If you're not getting any nibbles—especially if you've decided against using a Realtor—hold an open house. Advertise the open house a few days before the event in the classified section of your local paper (and online) and, if you like, with a yard sign. Make the house as attractive as possible and offer snacks throughout the day.

Pricing Your House

A real-estate agent can price your house for you or you can either price it yourself (keeping in mind that most people tend to overprice their homes), basing your estimate on similar homes you've seen for sale in your area, or hire an appraiser (this will cost you $50–$350). Pricing houses isn't an exact science, but if you start too high, you can always bring the price down, although by that time you may have scared some people away. If you start too low, you'll probably have a quick sale, but you may lose several thousands of dollars in the process.

Reviewing Your Offers

Reviewing offers is the fun part, assuming they're high enough for you to want to accept any of them. Most potential buyers expect to hear back in twenty-four hours, but you can take longer if you need to.

Be sure to read the offer carefully so you know everything the buyers expect you to leave or fix up. If you don't think an offer is high enough or you don't like some of the provisions and contingencies in the offer, you can propose a counteroffer. Be prepared, however, for the buyer to walk away upon reviewing your counteroffer.

Understanding Closing Expenses

Closing expenses (also called closing costs) are the expenses associated with transferring your property from you to your buyer. You pay these expenses at closing—a low-key event in which the buyer brings money and the seller gets money. Generally, closing costs for the buyer are added to the mortgage amount or paid as an additional down payment (although a few have to be paid before the closing), while closing costs for the seller are subtracted from the settlement check. Who pays what is up for negotiation. Sometimes an eager seller will offer to pay all of the buyer's closing costs. Most of the time, however, the buyer pays the majority of the closing costs:

- **Mortgage points.** Money paid by the buyer to lower the interest rate for the loan. (One point equals 1 percent of the loan amount.) When interest rates are low, few people pay points; when they're high, these costs can skyrocket.
- **Loan origination fee.** Administrative cost of processing the loan, paid by the buyer. Usually 1 to 2 percent of the loan amount.
- **Credit report.** Usually around $50, and may be paid by the buyer when the loan is first applied for.
- **Prepaid interest.** Interest owed by the buyer for the part of the month that comes after the closing date. Always try to close on the last day of the month so you won't owe any prepaid interest.
- **Escrow.** The first payment to the buyer's escrow account, which will collect monthly partial payments for insurance and property taxes and pay them when they're due.
- **Title Insurance.** A search to ensure that the seller actually owns the house. May be paid by seller or buyer.
- **Recording fee.** Fee to record the transfer of ownership. Often paid by the seller.

- **Appraisal.** Determines the estimated value of the house. Usually costs around $300 and may be due when the buyer applies for the loan.
- **Survey.** Determines the house's property lines; costs $150 to $350.
- **Pest inspection.** Ensures a pest-free (read that: termite-free) house and costs the buyer about $125.
- **Property taxes.** Most property taxes are paid one year after they are incurred, so you pay your 2008 property taxes in 2009. For this reason, the seller may have to pay six months' or a year's worth of property taxes to settle the bill.
- **Insurance-policy payment.** The buyer pays for one year of insurance in advance and/or brings proof that insurance for the house has been purchased.

Use **WORKSHEET 17-1** to estimate your closing costs. Your lender should give you an estimate early in the paperwork process.

WORKSHEET 17-1
Closing Expenses

Mortgage points	$
Loan-origination fee	$
Credit report	$
Prepaid interest	$
Escrow	$
Title insurance	$
Recording fee	$
Appraisal	$
Survey	$
Pest inspection	$
Property taxes	$
Insurance-policy payment	$
TOTAL:	$

Managing Unexpected Household Expenses

Chapter 13 gives you some advice on how to handle unexpected household expenses, and Chapter 10 describes how to refinance your mortgage and take cash out to pay for these expenses, so this section will be brief.

Generally, you'll want to put a little money away each month into a savings account and earmark it for household repairs. Even if you bought a brand-new, just-built house, at some point you'll have to repair loose shingles on the roof or upgrade the wiring, or whatever! Putting just $10 or $20 into an account each month will make those repairs so much easier to make. (Or course, if you bought a fixer-upper, you're going to want to put quite a bit more cash into savings for your many upcoming repairs.)

If you do end up needing a repair that wipes out your savings and gets your monthly financial obligations off track, contact your lender immediately. You may be able to take out some of the equity to pay for the repair, refinance your mortgage to include the repair costs, or just get an extra month to make your payment this time.

Creating a Budget That Includes Your New Home

You may have to make several changes to your budget in order to buy a new home. The first change includes saving for a down payment, while the second change—a few months or years later—will include your new monthly mortgage payment (including the extra you want to pay each month to pay it off early) and savings for repairs and maintenance. A third budget might show how you plan to change your spending after your house is paid off. Use **WORKSHEET** ¹⁷⁻² to work on your new budget(s).

If you do get into trouble and are facing foreclosure, beware of scam artists, often calling themselves mortgage consultants or foreclosure services, who offer to talk to your mortgage lender or intervene on your behalf to help you refinance. Not only will they charge you an upfront fee for this "service," they will often get the title to your home transferred to their company, pocket your fee, and then declare bankruptcy on your behalf.

WORKSHEET 17-2
A New-House Budget

Monthly Expense	Amount	Ways to Reduce/Eliminate	New Amount
Savings for down payment	$	N/A	$
Groceries and household items	$		$
Day care	$		$
Contributions	$		$
Savings	$		$
Rent on furniture or appliances	$		$
Entertainment/babysitting	$		$
Eating out	$		$
Rent or mortgage	$		$
Car payment or lease	$		$
Electric bill (average)	$		$
Gas bill (average)	$		$
Water bill	$		$
Sewer bill	$		$
Trash pick-up bill	$		$
Cable/DSL/satellite bill	$		$
Telephone bill	$		$
Cell-phone bill	$		$
Bank charges	$		$
Haircuts/manicures/pedicures	$		$
Home equity loan	$		$
Other loan	$		$
Credit card or store-charge bill	$		$
Credit card or store-charge bill	$		$
Credit card or store-charge bill	$		$

WORKSHEET 17-2

A New-House Budget (continued)

Monthly Expense	Amount	Ways to Reduce/Eliminate	New Amount
Credit card or store-charge bill	$		$
Credit card or store-charge bill	$		$
Child support or alimony	$		$
Car maintenance	$		$
House maintenance	$		$
Auto insurance	$		$
Property taxes	$		$
Gifts	$		$
Events to attend	$		$
Clothing and shoes	$		$
Home insurance	$		$
Vehicle registration	$		$
Vacation	$		$
Club membership	$		$
Other:	$		$
Other:	$		$
TOTAL:	$		$

Never let your mortgage get so far behind that your lender threatens foreclosure. You're much better off selling your house and moving to a smaller one that you can better afford (see Chapter 8) long before your situation ever gets to this point.

Chapter 18

Saving Money for College

Saving for college is on the lips and minds of nearly every parent in America. Although few people are actually able to save the total cost of tuition, fees, room, and board needed by college freshmen, the pressure of trying to do so is still stressful to parents. This chapter will help to reduce some of that stress.

Understanding College Costs

College costs can be a bit confusing; this section clears up what these costs are and what the average is today.

Tuition and Fees

This covers the salaries of professors, maintenance of buildings, use of school medical clinic, and so on. Basically, it's the cost of being a student (whether a commuter or resident) on a campus. At public colleges, this number is currently averaging just under $6,000 for in-state residents; it is over $22,000 for private schools, and about $2,300 per year for two-year public colleges.

Room and Board

Room and board includes a place to live and food to eat. Prices for tiny dorm rooms are exorbitant—room and board tends to cost between $7,000 and $8,000 per school year. You can usually save a bundle by living off campus, particularly if you share a rental house with other students.

FACT

Sometimes, parents with a bit of extra cash will buy a house for their college kids. The kids living there split the cost of the mortgage payment, taxes, and insurance (and often pay the same price they would if renting), and the parents sell the house when the kids graduate. It's really not a bad idea.

Books

College textbooks are expensive—textbooks can cost over $100 *each*. The average bill for books for a school year is about $900.

Study Abroad

Many college students try to take one semester or year and study abroad. Expenses vary by the student and the location, but this cost generally includes airfare to and from the location; tuition at the foreign school; and spending money at the location. However, when attending a very expensive university (such as Harvard, MIT, Notre Dame, and so on), studying abroad may actually cost *less,* even factoring in the increased travel costs.

Internships

Internships are becoming more and more vital to graduating college seniors. If you're able to work in your field of interest before graduation, you'll have a much easier time finding work in your field. Many students live at home while interning during summers; those who can't live at home will need to pay for an apartment during the internship period.

Transportation

Some freshman aren't allowed to have cars on campus, but if a student is to have any flexibility at all, taking a car to school—even an old clunker— is a good idea. You will, however, have to estimate gas, maintenance, insurance, excise or personal property taxes, and license. Transportation costs vary widely based on the cost of gas, but you can estimate about $1,000 per year for on-campus students and about $1,500 for commuters.

Some economists predict that college costs (tuition, fees, room, and board) will rise 6 percent per year, which means that current public-university tuition costs of, say, $6,000 per year, will rise to over $17,000 in eighteen years.

Miscellaneous Expenses

Miscellaneous expenses range from music downloads to late-night pizzas to gas. They generally run around $1,500 per year, for a student on a budget.

Determining How Much You Can (or Want to) Help Out

This isn't a subject that many people talk about, but at some point, you need to make a decision about how much you can or want to help your child pay for college. Paying for all of a child's college expenses is out of reach for many parents, and if you do so, it may make your child less able to appreciate the gift that attending college really is. A child who really wants to attend college will find a way, either by working part time, winning scholarships, or taking out loans.

Just as you can support your child financially, you can also support your child by visiting, calling, texting, sending e-mails, sending care packages, and so on. College can be quite lonely, especially during the first semester, and your emotional support will surely help.

Don't assume that you and your spouse or partner feel the same way about whether to pay your kid's college expenses. While you want to try to come to a consensus, agreeing to disagree is okay, too.

Also be sure to include your growing child in this conversation. Kids who expect to pay for all or part of college will be better equipped to deal with finding money than will kids who assume money is available and then are told later that full support is not available.

Seeing How Much You Can Save

How much you can save for your child depends on three factors: How much you're able to invest; how long you have; and how much you can earn in interest. In general, investing a small amount each month for eighteen years will yield greater savings than investing larger amounts for four or five years. **TABLE 18-1** gives some examples of what you'd save if you put money for college in a tax-free or tax-deferred account.

To find out how much you can save for your child's college fund, visit the FinAid site at *www.finaid.org* and click on their Calculators section. You can play around with the numbers and determine how much you can save over time.

TABLE 18-1

Saving for College

Monthly Deposit	Interest Rate	Number of Years	Total Savings
$25	5%	5	$1,707.24
$25	5%	18	$8,766.43
$165	5%	18	$57,858.41
$165	2%	18	$42,928.53
$165	9%	18	$89,161.77
$500	5%	3	$19,457.41
$500	5%	18	$175,328.52

Taking Advantage of Government-Sponsored Savings Plans

If you have eighteen years to save for college, chances are you'll end up with quite a bit of money for your child. But even if you don't have that much time, three tax-free college-savings vehicles can help you save for your child's college expenses. Between the grants that are available to students and the tax savings you can realize, the government can actually be a big help to you and your child. On average, students receive more than $3,000 in grants and tax benefits at public four-year colleges; $9,000 per year at private four-year schools; and $2,200 per year (or nearly the entire amount of tuition) at two-year colleges.

Coverdell Education Savings Accounts

Although renamed the Coverdell education savings accounts several years ago, these are still often called by their old name: Education IRAs. These accounts allow you to contribute $2,000 per year, tax free, for college. (Keep in mind, however, that unless Congress extends the plan, 2010 will bring many changes to the plan, including a much lower annual contribution.) The withdrawals are tax free, too. The account is in the name of the child (called the beneficiary), and nearly anyone can contribute to it tax free, including grandparents, godparents, aunts and uncles, and you, up to the maximum amount each year. Contributing more than the maximum amount, even from several different sources, can result in penalties.

FACT

The tax savings for contributing to Coverdell accounts begins to phase out at $95,000 in income for individuals and $190,000 for couples. That's a lot of income, yes, and probably doesn't apply to you, but if other family members or friends want to contribute to your child's IRA, they should be aware that there are income limits on who can receive the tax break.

The money in Coverdell accounts can be used not only for college tuition, fees, room, board, and books, but also for an education-related computer, academic tutoring, and transportation to and from school. The money can also be used for K–12 expenses, including private-school tuition. If the funds aren't used for education, the account remains in the name of the beneficiary—it doesn't revert back to you or the other donors, and this might really grind your gears.

There's only one catch, really: The funds must be used within a month of your child turning thirty years old. If money were ever left in a Coverdell account and your child turned thirty plus a month, he or she could start another account in the name of another child. This does mean, however, that Coverdell accounts aren't very useful for older adults who want to return to college.

Okay, there's kind of another catch, too. The financial institution that holds your Coverdell account will charge the account a maintenance fee for managing the investment account. The fee is usually small, however.

529s: College Savings Plans

All U.S. states currently sponsor college-savings investment plans. Currently, money put into a state-sponsored 529 is tax free upon withdrawal, and some states give a tax break when you contribute to the plan, too. Beginning in 2010, however, withdrawals will be taxed at the child's current tax rate.

The fact that states sponsor the plans (and may give state income-tax breaks on the deposits) leads some people to believe that your child has to attend an in-state public university in order to use the funds. Only state-sponsored prepaid-tuition plans have that requirement (see the following section); funds in 529 college-savings plans can be used at any college or university in the country.

Basically, the plans operate very much like an education IRA, except that instead of the money being owned and controlled by the child, 529s are owned and controlled by the parent. Your child is still the named beneficiary, but he or she has no legal right to the money if you choose not to authorize a withdrawal. And you can change the named beneficiary at any time. Anyone can contribute to the 529 fund.

Another striking difference between an education IRA and a 529 is that the amount you can contribute to a 529 is virtually limitless, with no loss of tax benefits for high-income donors. Also, the plan doesn't stop at age thirty, so you can establish one for yourself to earn your first degree or attend graduate school.

QUESTION?

How can I get information about my state's plan?
The Saving for College Web site at *www.savingforcollege.com* lists every 529 savings plan administered in the country, and then reviews information about the plan's manager and its investment rating.

The tax implications of 529s are not easy to understand. If you're already using the services of a tax accountant, be sure to discuss your college-savings plan, too. If not, consider hiring a qualified tax accountant to help you wade through the many regulations covering these plans.

The account is placed in the hands of an investment-fund manager who charges a maintenance fee, and you can establish direct-deposit funds into the account, making deposits to the plan simple and relatively painless.

Another Kind of 529: Prepaid Tuition Plans

A prepaid-tuition plan allows you to buy tuition shares or units and then hold on to those shares until your child wants to use them. Buying a share is just like paying tuition, but at today's prices. You lock in at today's tuition rates, thus avoiding the dreaded annual increase in tuition. Family members and friends can buy shares for your child, too, but some states require contracts that lock you in to buying a certain number of shares in a given period of time.

When your child receives the prepaid-tuition shares to use to pay for college, the federal government usually taxes them as income. Since your child has a low tax rate, it may still result in tax savings. States don't usually tax prepaid-tuition shares.

The plans vary greatly in where and how they can be used. Some colleges and universities sell tuition shares directly, but they can be used only at that school. In other cases, states sell the shares, and they can be used at any public—and sometimes private—college in that state. Some blocks of schools (like a group of private schools) sell the share. If your child decides not to attend that college or isn't accepted at one, you may be eligible for a refund of the tuition shares, but often a penalty is levied. If you purchased the shares directly from the college or university, you may be able to sell them to another family to use.

Finding Other Ways to Pay for College

The tax-free savings plans discussed in the preceding section are great if you have a few thousand dollars a year to invest for your child. If you're not able to squeeze that much out of your budget, however, consider the following ways to help your child pay for college.

A Fifteen-Year Home Mortgage

One creative way to pay for college if you don't currently have the money to do so is to buy a house (or refinance an existing house) on a fifteen-year mortgage when your child is born. When you pay off the house fifteen years later, begin putting that "mortgage payment" into a savings account or low-risk investment fund.

The account will have thirty-six "mortgage payments" in it by the time the child is ready for college—an amount that, depending on your mortgage payment, could be substantial. At 5-percent interest, a $1,000-per-month "mortgage payment" into your savings account will yield $38,914.81 in three years. You can then continue using what was mortgage money for college money throughout your child's four or five years at college.

Scholarships and Grants

Scholarships range from athletic grants to academic scholarships to money that's based on geography or heritage. Peruse the many money-for-college books at your local library, and encourage your child to apply for any and every scholarship that looks appropriate.

The majority of academic scholarships now offered to college-bound seniors are based on scores received on the PSAT and SAT. Because only the best scores are reported, encourage your child to take the test early and often, perhaps even investing in a study course. While the tests and study courses do cost money, they could add up to tens of thousands of dollars in scholarships if your child scores among the top students in the country. Some colleges even offer free tuition and fees for students who score a perfect or nearly perfect mark.

To become eligible for any government grants or loans, your child must complete a Free Application for Federal Student Aid (FAFSA). This form can be time-consuming to complete and may include information that you would rather keep private. Still, no government grants or loans are given unless this form is on file.

The most well-known college grant is the federal Pell Grant, which gives money (up to $4,050) directly to low-income children attending college. It does not have to be repaid, and is available only to undergraduates earning their first degree. Federal Supplemental Educational Opportunity Grants, which range from $100 to $4,000, may also be available to low-income students.

Loans

Loans are different from scholarships and grants in that they must be repaid after the child graduates from or stops attending college. Federal student loans are usually borrowed directly from the government or from qualifying private lenders—both offer an attractive low interest rate. Many families, even those that do not appear to demonstrate much of a need, are eligible for federal student loans.

Federal Perkins Loans are borrowed directly from the school (also at a low interest rate), but are available only for low-income students. You can borrow up to $4,000 per year for undergraduate study. Federal Family Education Loans (FFEL) and the William D. Ford Federal Direct Loan are administered by the U.S. Department of Education as either Stafford Loans or PLUS loans. Stafford Loans are available directly to students, and may or may not be based on need. Total loans vary from $3,500 per year to $10,500 per year for undergrads. PLUS loans are available to the parents of college-bound students, but instead of being due when the child graduates, they must be repaid while the child is still in school.

Work Study and Other Jobs

A lot of students work while in college, and not only does working often not hurt the student's chances of succeeding, it can actually improve his or her chances of being hired after college! Working forces students to be disciplined, and also may provide real-life experience (especially when doing a co-op or internship) that can make a resume shine.

Here are some broad categories of work opportunities for your child:

- **Work study.** Federal work-study programs allow students with financial need to be employed, usually by the university or surrounding community, for a certain number of hours per week. This option is considered part of a student's financial-aid package, along with grants and loans.
- **Part-time job.** A student can apply for a job at the bagel shop or as a professor's assistant and is usually paid minimum wage.
- **Full-time job.** Your child can opt to work full time and attend school part time. Although the full-time job usually isn't professional work, the company may offer some tuition assistance or a flexible work schedule built around class schedules. Most students take six to ten years to finish a degree while working full time.
- **Co-operative education.** A college co-op education alternates semesters of full-time college attendance with semesters of full-time work in the student's field of interest. The semesters of work usually pay quite well—sometimes enough to pay all of the student's college expenses, plus living expenses during the work semesters. Co-op positions are difficult to get, and they're demanding because the student must behave professionally during the work semesters and must take full course loads while at school. Most co-op students graduate in five years. Because of their real-life experiences, however, students who co-op are usually the first ones hired upon graduation.
- **Internship.** An internship is similar to a co-op, except that students usually attend their eight semesters of school like other students, interning only during summers and other school breaks. Unfortunately, some internships pay poorly or not at all, but they do provide necessary real-world job experience.

Creating a Budget That Includes College Expenses

In order to begin saving for your child's (or your own) college expenses—whether you have eighteen years or eighteen months—you'll need to sharpen your pencil and rework your budget. First, look at your budget to see how much you might be able to pull together each month by reducing your expenses. Then visit *www.finaid.org* to determine how much you'll be able to save.

WORKSHEET 18-2

A Child-in-College Budget

Monthly Expense	Amount	Ways to Reduce/Eliminate	New Amount
College costs	$	N/A	$
Groceries and household items	$		$
Day care	$		$
Contributions	$		$
Savings	$		$
Rent on furniture or appliances	$		$
Entertainment/babysitting	$		$
Eating out	$		$
Rent or mortgage	$		$
Car payment or lease	$		$
Electric bill (average)	$		$
Gas bill (average)	$		$
Water bill	$		$
Sewer bill	$		$
Trash pick-up bill	$		$
Cable/DSL/satellite bill	$		$
Telephone bill	$		$
Cell-phone bill	$		$

WORKSHEET 18-2
A Child-in-College Budget (*continued*)

Monthly Expense	Amount	Ways to Reduce/Eliminate	New Amount
Bank charges	$		$
Haircuts/manicures/pedicures	$		$
Home equity loan	$		$
Other loan	$		$
Credit card or store-charge bill	$		$
Credit card or store-charge bill	$		$
Credit card or store-charge bill	$		$
Credit card or store-charge bill	$		$
Credit card or store-charge bill	$		$
Credit card or store-charge bill	$		$
Child support or alimony	$		$
Car maintenance	$		$
House maintenance	$		$
Auto insurance	$		$
Property taxes	$		$
Gifts	$		$
Events to attend	$		$
Clothing and shoes	$		$
Home insurance	$		$
Vehicle registration	$		$
Vacation	$		$
Club membership	$		$
Other:	$		$
Other:	$		$
TOTAL:	$		$

Another way to determine your savings is to ignore the fact that you'll be earning interest on your money, and just multiply your monthly contribution by the number of months you have between now and the time your child will start college. Compare that number to today's tuition, fees, room, and board, and you'll have a good idea of how much college your savings will buy. The reason this method works fairly well is that college costs are rising by about the same amount that most investments are yielding.

The FedMoney site (*www.fedmoney.org*) lists dozens of government programs that give students money for college. If you've been thinking that you can't afford college, visit this site before you give up! There are other sites, too: Search on the phrase "college scholarships."

If you're not satisfied with your potential savings, see if you can find extra money in your budget (by cutting back even further on your expenses), and then calculate how much you'll have saved by putting away that amount (see **WORKSHEET** 18-2).

Chapter 19

Budgeting Through a Separation or Divorce

Unfortunately, in spite of our best intentions, approximately one out of every two marriages ends in divorce. If you're a part of the 50 percent that never has to go through the breakup of a marriage, consider yourself extremely fortunate. But if you do go through a divorce, remember that the situation does get better, with time. Both separation and divorce are emotionally and financially taxing, but give yourself two to five years, and both your heart and your pocketbook really will heal. This chapter can help you with the pocketbook portion of your healing journey.

Keeping a Level Head During a Difficult Time

During a divorce or separation, perhaps the toughest of times, it's important to keep a cool head. If that's not your nature, meet regularly (daily, even) with a friend or counselor who can help you talk through your frustrations and fears.

Generally, the biggest fear is that of women who haven't been working outside the home and don't know how they're going to handle their finances in the weeks and months ahead. If this sounds like you, be sure to complete the budget at the end of this chapter, and then sit down with your spouse and/or lawyer, and determine what funds you can tap to pay your daily expenses.

Although this divorce may force you to return to the work world sooner than you expected, the initial days following the decision to divorce is *not* the time to start job hunting. Preparing a resume, targeting the right companies, writing cover letters, and going on interviews is stressful enough, but at this time in your life, it could send you over the edge. Instead, for the short term, focus on finding ways to access some funds, and whether your spouse is required by law to continue to pay your joint bills, even if you're no longer living together.

Also take care of your children. This may be a miserable time for them, so they need both you and your spouse to be available to answer questions and to guide and support them. If funds allow, try to let their lives continue as planned: If they were going to attend horse camp this summer, work to keep that possible, in spite of the divorce proceedings.

FACT

Studies show that children of parents who are in violent or otherwise abusive marriages fare better after their parents divorce than they do when their parents stay married. Staying in a bad relationship for the sake of your children is rarely good for your children.

Splitting One Household into Two

Generally, when a couple divorces, they first separate. In fact, in some states, couples are not allowed to divorce until they have first separated—in some cases, for as long as six months or a year. In other states, however, a lengthy separation is not required.

Generally, the person asking for the divorce moves out of the household, but that is not always the case. If one spouse will be retaining the majority of the custody of the children, that spouse may keep the house, even if he or she requested the divorce. Regardless of who's staying where—and even whether the house will eventually be sold or will be kept by one of the spouses—one spouse probably has to find a place to stay and get some furnishings. In other words, you have to start operating as two households, which are separate financial entities.

Finding a New Place to Live, Even Temporarily

You have several options as you look for a place to live during a separation: Stay in a hotel; bunk with a friend or with family; rent a place of your own; buy a place of your own.

What's best for you depends on your financial situation, but in general, your best bet is a long-term hotel option (provided it's not lavishly expensive) or a short-term rental (with a six-month or one-year lease, at most). Staying with a friend or family generally leads to problems; most people choose this option because they're sure their relationship problems will resolve, thus they don't want to commit to any longer-term option. But most separations are not temporary, which leaves the person who's bunking with a friend living in limbo, hoping for reconciliation instead of healing and moving on. In addition, although separation is a deeply sad time for most people, it is also a time for intense self-reflection, a process that is difficult to enter and sustain if a roommate or housemate is always around. If you choose this option, before you move in, set an end date—perhaps two or three weeks in the future—that your friend agrees with.

Buying a place is also not a terrific option, mainly because you're not likely to be in a state to be making sound long-term decisions. (Incidentally, this is also why remarrying within the first two years of a divorce is not a good idea.) You're better off finding a place of your own that you can temporarily call home. From that base, you can begin to look for more permanent housing, perhaps six months, a year, or longer from the time you first move.

ALERT!

Be sure to keep paying the mortgage on your house, even if only one of you (or neither of you) is living there anymore. You don't want to ruin your credit rating by defaulting on a mortgage.

Furnishings and Other Necessities

Unless you move into a furnished apartment or hotel, you're going to need to set up your household, and this can be a budget buster. You'll take with you your clothes, perhaps some of your books and DVDs, and maybe a few personal items like a laptop or iPod. Eventually, you may also split up your furnishings, but at first, it may just be you and your clothes, which means you need a bed, dresser, living-room furniture, dining table or other place to eat, bookshelves, pots and pans, dishes, silverware, beddings, towels, and the like. And this all adds up!

ESSENTIAL

One exception to this rule is your mattress: Buy the best you can afford. You don't want to spend the next year or two tossing and turning or developing back problems by buying a cheap mattress. Shop sales at the big mattress warehouses, and also check out the higher-end selections at wholesale clubs like Sam's and Costco.

Although you may think your best bet is to buy high-quality items that will last for years, the opposite is usually true at this time. Instead, consider everything you buy at this time to be fairly temporary, because your tastes, desires, and needs may change radically over the next year or two. So, go for the minimalist approach, shopping at garage sales for furnishings (which you can paint in order to spruce up) and going discount for just about everything else. In a year or two, when you start to feel comfortable in your new singleness, you can slowly start to acquire higher-quality pieces.

Bank Accounts and Credit Cards

Before your divorce can be finalized, you'll need to separate your bank accounts, credit cards, and other loans. If you don't have a balance on your cards, you can simply decide who gets which cards, and take the other's name off by calling the credit card companies. Many credit card companies will also issue a separate credit card (one with a different account number) to the spouse who is not the primary card holder.

If you do carry a balance, however, that account will become part of your divorce settlement, either to be paid out of the proceeds of selling the house, or to be paid by one of the two of you. When the card is paid off, it can either be cancelled or it can revert to the primary card holder's name.

If you're a woman and want to return to your maiden name after a divorce, you'll need to keep your divorce paperwork handy during the name-change process, because it will show your intention to restore your name. Start with your state's motor-vehicles division to get a new driver's license, and then visit your bank. From there, call your credit card companies, mortgage company, insurance companies, frequent-flier and hotel-stay clubs, and so on. Apply for a new passport, too. Some folks may need you to fax your divorce paperwork; others will simply change the name as soon as you call or visit.

Keeping Expenses Under Control During the First Year

It's exceedingly common for people to go into debt during the first year of a separation or divorce. Part of the reason is the transitory nature of the separation; the unanswered questions: Will you get back together? Will the house fetch a fantastic price? Will you meet someone wonderful—and wealthy?

These unknowns, combined with sudden and unexpected expenses, can quickly lead to debt.

For many people, especially those who have been married a long time, divorce also represents a time to express long-hidden aspects of one's personality. So, many people who are newly separated finally buy that convertible sports car or spring for a new wardrobe. Why? Because they can, darn it!

Yes, you absolutely can. And maybe, in some ways, you need to find ways to assert who you are during this time of change and uncertainty. But as any good therapist will tell you, chances are, anything you buy during the first year or two after your divorce will tend to be whatever your ex-spouse hated, not necessarily what you like or want. If your ex-spouse hated purple or yellow, you may decide to decorate lavishly in both colors—even if your favorite is really green—just to stick it to him or her.

So, your best bet for your financial picture is to spend cautiously during this time. You don't want to end up with a lot of yellow and purple that you then have to live with for another decade. Worse, you don't want to end up broke or deeply in debt when all you really needed was time to grieve, heal, and move forward. The solution? Identify your essential expenses in **WORKSHEET 19-1.** For anything else, keep a list of items you'd like to purchase exactly two years after your divorce is final. Save up for those items, and on the two-year anniversary of your divorce, go crazy. By that time, you'll likely have had time to heal, get a better handle on who you are, and understand where your personal tastes lie.

Hiring (and Budgeting for) Legal Counsel

The average legal fees for a divorce range $1,500–$5,000 (for each person) for a simple divorce; a complicated divorce can run $20,000 or more.

Nearly all of the costs are paid to lawyers—the actual court costs for filing a divorce run only a few hundred dollars in most states. So, to substantially cut your costs, you can file for a divorce without using the services of an attorney. This approach has its pros and cons, however:

Not using an attorney will likely save you a lot money; however, if you're not well acquainted with the law, you may not negotiate very well on your own behalf. If you just want to get out of the marriage, no matter what the cost, you're probably better off hiring an attorney. Likewise, if your spouse can easily manipulate you, you're also better off with a lawyer. In these cases, you may sign off on more than you likely should. If you're representing yourself in a divorce, keep in mind that in most states, you're entitled to half of the marital assets (house, savings accounts) and are responsible for half of the marital debts (mortgage, credit cards). You may also be eligible for a portion of your spouse's retirement benefits and medical benefits (whether or not you have children). If you worked while your spouse attended graduate, medical, or law school, you may also be eligible for a portion of his or her lifelong earnings.

Using an attorney may get you a more equitable settlement. Although you'll pay through the nose for attorney's fees, your settlement may be higher in the end than if you had negotiated the divorce on your own, especially if you hire a good attorney. So, although you have to pay more now, you may end up with a better financial situation in the long run. However, remember that attorneys are not tied emotionally to your spouse and may create additional acrimony in your relationship. If you use an attorney, keep in mind that your attorney represents you. If he or she is doing or asking for anything with which you don't agree, stop your attorney and restate your wishes. If your attorney persists in acting in ways that don't fit your value system or even that make you uncomfortable, consider hiring someone else to take your case.

One compromise that is gaining favor is to hire an attorney as a consultant, calling on him or her to give you specific advice at specific times during the divorce. You handle the paperwork and do all the negotiating with your soon-to-be-ex, but when you're unsure of the legal implications of anything you're doing, your on-call legal consultant is available for your call or visit, and charges you an hourly fee.

Aren't lawyers the reason divorces get so nasty?
If you're convinced that lawyers are always the cause of bad feelings in a divorce, think again. Couples who go it alone, resolving to remain good friends and have an amicable divorce, can still experience bitter feelings, especially when one spouse or the other experiences happy tidings in the future: remarriage, children, new house, and so on.

Another solution is to handle your own divorce, but hire a mediator (who is either a counselor or an attorney) for any issues that don't appear to be resolvable. A mediator usually charges $100–$200 per hour, but mediation sessions tend to resolve issues quickly.

Understanding the Impact of Alimony and Child Support

Even if you're sure you're going to receive alimony (which is rare) and/or child support (which you receive only if your children are under age 18 and live with you more than 50 percent of the time), you probably won't start receiving payments until after your divorce is final, and even then, they may not arrive on time.

If possible, *don't* count on alimony or child support. Instead, plan how you're going to support yourself without those sources of income, and if or when they do arrive, deposit the checks into a savings account for your children. They can eventually use that money for summer camps, a car, college tuition, and so on. You and/or your children are due this money, but if you can construct a financial life that doesn't rely on these sources of income, do so, and treat these payments as additional income that will eventually pay off handsomely for your children.

Taking Time Before Committing to Another Relationship

For all the reasons that you don't want to buy a house or a convertible, you also don't want to commit to another relationship right after a separation or divorce. Post-divorce romances tend to go something like this:

1. **"I can't be alone...I must find someone!"** This may last anywhere from a few weeks to a few months (or, in some cases, years), but it tends to be the initial response after the reality of separation or divorce sinks in. In fact, some people are so sure they can't be alone that they find someone *before* a crumbling marriage ends. If this phase sounds like where you are, seek out a support group or therapist who can help you become comfortable with living alone, at least during your separation or divorce.

2. **"Marriage? Ewww. No way."** As the divorce is finalized—and especially if one spouse was financially disadvantaged in the divorce—feelings of "never, ever again" may quickly surface. This is common, but it generally doesn't last. So, don't worry too much about these feeling, but also don't make any irreversible decisions during this time (such as having a vasectomy) that may be the result of a phase rather than a true lifelong desire.

3. **"I just want to play."** Casual dating tends to come next. This is when dating people who are emotionally or intellectually incompatible tends to happen. During this phase, whatever you do, *don't* get married or give away money. It is extraordinarily rare for this person to actually end up being right for you. One divorce is bad enough, but jumping into another relationship that is almost assured of going south will likely lead to a second, and that's doubly hard. ***Note:*** Phases 2 and 3 may be reversed or may even occur at the same time!

4. **"I could see myself getting married again, but I would miss being single, too."** Now you're ready to date seriously. If you've developed such strong social networks and such a pleasant home life for yourself that you would miss your singleness, yet at the same time you can envision meeting and marrying the right person, you're likely ready to consider entering a long-term relationship.

Creating a Single-Again Budget

This chapter helps prepare you to be single once again. Chances are, your finances will be tight, but you can find ways to stay within a budget as you look for separate housing, find comfortable furnishings, and pay for legal costs.

WORKSHEET 19-1

Single-Again Budget

Monthly Expense	Amount	Ways to Reduce/Eliminate	New Amount
Groceries and household items	$		$
Contributions	$		$
Savings	$		$
Day care	$		$
Rent on furniture or appliances	$		$
Entertainment/babysitting	$		$
Eating out	$		$
Rent or mortgage	$		$
Car payment or lease	$		$
Electric bill (average)	$		$
Gas bill (average)	$		$
Water bill	$		$
Sewer bill	$		$
Trash pick-up bill	$		$
Cable/DSL/satellite bill	$		$
Telephone bill	$		$
Cell-phone bill	$		$
Bank charges	$		$
Haircuts/manicures/pedicures	$		$
Home equity loan	$		$

WORKSHEET 19-1
Single-Again Budget (*continued*)

Monthly Expense	Amount	Ways to Reduce/Eliminate	New Amount
Other loan	$		$
Credit card or store-charge bill	$		$
Credit card or store-charge bill	$		$
Credit card or store-charge bill	$		$
Credit card or store-charge bill	$		$
Credit card or store-charge bill	$		$
Credit card or store-charge bill	$		$
Credit card or store-charge bill	$		$
Child support or alimony	$		$
Car maintenance	$		$
House maintenance	$		$
Auto insurance	$		$
Property taxes	$		$
Gifts	$		$
Events to attend	$		$
Clothing and shoes	$		$
Home insurance	$		$
Vehicle registration	$		$
Vacation	$		$
Club membership	$		$
Other:	$		$
Other:	$		$
TOTAL:	$		$

Chapter 20

Changing Your Budget After Age Fifty

Life after fifty can be a delightful time. You can often begin to do more for yourself at the same time that you're financially better equipped to help others. As you near or enter retirement, however, you may also find yourself bearing responsibility for your aging parents or for your grandchildren. This chapter helps you adjust your budget to meet these challenges.

Determining How Much You Want to Assist Your Grown Children

One of the biggest questions—and, potentially, frustrations—facing you today may be how much you want to help your grown children live their lives. Increasingly, and especially during economic downturns, older Americans find themselves answering the front door and encountering their grown children, wanting to move back in or receive other financial assistance.

Even as you enter your fifties, your children may be nowhere near grown. If you had children in your late thirties or early forties, you may still have preteens around the house. If so, much of this chapter may not apply to you until you near sixty or sixty-five.

This need for assistance on the part of your children may frustrate you on a number of levels. First, you probably did not move back in with your parents after you left home, and you don't understand why anyone would find this necessary. Second, you may have observed your children making poor financial decisions over the years and not feel a great responsibility to bail them out. Third, you may have paid for all or a large part of your child's college education and believe that you have done enough to get your child started in life. Finally, you may have been looking forward to turning your attention inward, both emotionally and financially, and resent that your children are still so needy.

Knowing Why Your Children Need You So Much

As a baby boomer, you were part of the first generation of Americans that, as a whole, planned for and attended college, graduated, found productive and high-paying jobs, and as you entered your middle years, were able to buy houses and brand-new cars with relative ease. Your generation was, therefore, better off than the generation before, which was better off than the generation before it.

This is not to say that your life and career have been easy. Your parents probably did not pay for your college education (if you were able to go at all), and you had to work very, very hard to afford the life you've lived. You survived several recessions and waves of layoffs. You've made a lot of sacrifices and done without so that your children would have a good life.

Unfortunately, because you provided so well for your children, they have grown up with almost no hope of doing better than your generation, and this is an unusual phenomenon. They've grown accustomed to a lifestyle during childhood that they can't afford as adults. Children of boomers who go away to college aren't excited by the prospect of living in a dorm; they're horrified by the lack of closet space and missing amenities. They don't understand how much personal electronics and a new car actually cost. Yet as they graduate from college and seek jobs, many haven't been able to find jobs that pay enough to support the lifestyle that they grew accustomed to when they lived with you.

FACT

Today, houses cost far more as a percentage of income than they did when you were a young man or woman. If you sold your house recently, weren't you amazed that the house you paid $30,000 for is now worth $500,000? Well, your kids are amazed, too, when they try to buy houses like yours.

So, they've gotten themselves into massive debt trying to replicate the life you've had. They finance their houses on thirty- or fifty-year loans with no hope of ever paying them off, lease cars that they can't afford, and put most of their purchases on credit cards and store charges. And when those debts become overwhelming, they simply refinance their houses for another thirty years and start fresh. This may have left your children with little ability to live within a budget, no equity in their houses, and an overwhelming desire to consume instead of save. So they turn to you for help, and you need to decide how much you want to give. Use **WORKSHEET** ²⁰⁻¹ to brainstorm ways that you might be interested in helping your children.

WORKSHEET 20-1

How Do You Want to Assist Your Grown Children?

Type of Assistance	Potential Cost	Monthly Savings to Add to Budget
	$	$
	$	$
	$	$
	$	$
	$	$
	$	$
	$	$
	$	$
	$	$
	$	$

Helping Financially

Helping your children financially may range from bailing them out of credit card debt to paying for another college degree to giving them a down payment on a house. If you're able and willing to offer this kind of assistance, your kids will surely appreciate it. They may, however, continue to live above their means and wreak financial havoc on themselves and those around them.

Therefore, if you do offer to help your children financially, attach some strings, just as a credit-counseling agency or bankruptcy court does. Insist on getting a budget from your child that includes paying off all debt and putting money into savings over the next few years. At that time—and not before!—offer to give your child a down payment on a house or money to go back to school.

If your child and a spouse are going to move in with you, use adherence to a strict budget as the ticket to continuing this free rent. If they don't stick to a budget, they have to move out. You may even want to collect rent from them, put it into a savings account, and give it back to them when they are ready to move out. And do set a time limit on how long your grown children can live with you.

You may hear from your kids that because they didn't like their jobs, they quit, and they're now experiencing moderate to severe financial difficulties. Before you blow your top, keep in mind that personal satisfaction is much more highly rated now than it was when you were working at your first few jobs. Putting happiness in front of earnings is admirable; in fact, it may be something you've never done, and your child may need to hear this from you. However, your grown child also needs to realize that a price comes with that commitment to his or her own happiness: Living a much more frugal lifestyle. Being a social worker or teacher may bring much more satisfaction than using the law degree that you helped pay for, but it also means your child is going to have to embrace an entirely different lifestyle.

Don't get sucked into helping more than you want to. Your children may not realize that you don't necessarily want to spend every spare moment with your grandchildren. If your children begin to rely on you for this service, they may grow even more dependent on you.

Helping financially, and holding your kids accountable as you do so, doesn't mean you can't also give financial gifts that have no strings attached. Giving a check or a beautiful piece of furniture for a birthday or holiday gift will probably make you feel fantastic.

Helping with Child Care

If you have the desire and time to help babysit your grandchildren, you may benefit doubly: You get to help your child while spending time with your grandkids. Decide up front, however, whether you want your assistance to be official, perhaps in the daytime while your child works, or unofficial, such as babysitting your grandchildren while their parents shop or enjoy a night out alone.

Taking Care of Your Aging Parents

Another difficult decision you may soon face is how and how much to help your aging parents. The following sections discuss the two more popular solutions.

Paying for Their Care

If your parent becomes unable to live without assistance, you may need to bring in someone to assist with everyday tasks. This may be a person who visits or lives with your parent at home, or it may mean that your parent moves to a nursing facility.

Either way, the service can be astronomically expensive, and far too many children raid their retirement accounts or tap the equity in their homes to pay for their parents' care. The thinking is this: "I'm responsible for my parents; therefore, I must pay all of their expenses, regardless of the consequences." This way of thinking is absolutely correct, except for the part about disregarding the consequences. Always put your financial security first. When your financial needs are met, give as much as you possibly can to the people you want to help, which may well include your parents.

Before you tap any of your own resources, check to see what resources your parents have. While you may prefer to keep your mother's house because she hopes to move back there someday, if her nursing care costs $40,000 per year, she may not have that luxury. In the same way, while your father had hoped to live off the interest on his retirement fund instead of tapping the principal (the actual amount in the account), that plan may have to change if he needs special care. And always look into what benefits Social Security and Medicare provide for your parents.

Inviting Them to Live with You

An alternative to paying for a nursing home or in-home aid to care for your parent is to have him or her move in with you. If you have the space and, for the most part, enjoy the company of your parent, this may be a useful arrangement.

It will not, however, be a free arrangement. If your parent requires care, you may not be able to work or you may have to split shifts with your spouse. In addition, your expenses for food and utilities will likely increase. And if your parent doesn't have medical insurance, you may be expected to foot the bill for prescriptions and doctor visits.

If you find yourself responsible for your parents' welfare and you have brothers and sisters, insist that they share part of the burden. Too many family members allow one sibling to take full responsibility for a parent—including, potentially, the economic responsibility—without ever offering to help.

As mentioned in the preceding section, don't let your parents' resources sit unused. It is your parents' responsibility to pay for their own care as long as possible. If you tap your own retirement account or home equity to pay for your parents' care, you'll end up forcing your children to have the same responsibility for you.

Helping Your Grandchildren Financially

One of the great joys of your life may be your grandchildren, and you may want to help them financially as much as possible. The following sections outline a few common areas of financial assistance; use **WORKSHEET 20-2** to brainstorm additional ways to help.

WORKSHEET 20-2
How Much Do You Want to Help Your Grandchildren?

Type of Assistance	Potential Cost	Monthly Savings to Add to Budget
	$	$
	$	$
	$	$
	$	$
	$	$
	$	$

Paying Some College Costs

If your grandchildren's parents haven't already established a college savings account (including the tax-free ones listed in Chapter 18), you may want to do that for your grandchild. You can then contribute regularly to it and in this way assist with his or her college costs.

Buying a Car

As your grandchild approaches the legal driving age, you may be tempted to buy him or her a car. If the child's parents approve and you can afford it, giving a car is an extremely thoughtful way to help your grandchild.

However, to avoid having your grandchild face the same financial problems that his or her parents may face, you may want to steer clear of luxury or sports cars. A used, safe, midsize or economy car (or, better yet, high-mpg hybrid car) will be a welcome gift that won't set your grandchild up for financial disappointment later in life.

Helping with a Down Payment on a House

As your grandchild enters young adulthood, you may want to help him or her save for a down payment on a house. However, instead of giving a handout, consider creating a Grandma or Grandpa Matching Fund. Each month your grandchild sends you a set amount of money to save toward a down payment. Each month you put that check, plus a check of your own for the same amount, into a savings or investment account that's in the names of both you and your grandchild. When the account grows to a certain amount, your grandchild can withdraw it and use it as a down payment on a house. This way you'll teach your grandchild a great deal about saving and budgeting, and you'll be helping out but won't be providing a no-strings-attached gift.

Doing More for Yourself

The second half of your life is a fantastic time to think about and pursue the activities, careers, educational goals, and business opportunities you've always thought about. Use **WORKSHEET 20-3** to brainstorm these activities and review the following sections for some ideas.

WORKSHEET 20-3

What Changes Do You Want (or Need) to Make in Your Life?

Change	Potential Cost	Monthly Savings to Add to Budget
	$	$
	$	$
	$	$
	$	$
	$	$
	$	$
	$	$
	$	$
	$	$
	$	$
	$	$
	$	$

Traveling

If you've always wanted to travel the world and now have the time and resources to do it, fine-tune your budget to find ways to pay for it. Traveling after age fifty-five is especially cost effective because many hotels, tour companies, restaurants, and attractions give generous senior-citizen discounts.

Going Back to School

Going back to college for a degree after age fifty isn't embarrassing or silly, it's a fantastic way to enrich your life. Some colleges even offer discounts for older students, and you can use the tips in Chapter 18 to find ways to pay for your tuition and fees.

What if I don't live near a college?
You can take college courses even if you don't live anywhere near a college campus. Look into short summer sessions (six or eight weeks) that could be a fun break from home. And check out low-residency and distance-education programs that allow you to learn at home.

Exploring New Career Options

After fifty is a great time to change careers or start a business. Just be sure that you save in advance for any reduction in income that you might experience! See Chapter 11 for some basic information on starting a business.

Assessing Your Retirement Income and Expenses

If you're planning to live on retirement income, you'll want to continually assess the value of your retirement portfolio (see Chapter 21) and find ways to cut back on your expenses, if necessary. **WORKSHEETS** 20-4 and 20-5 can help you total your expected income and brainstorm ideas for reducing your expenses.

WORKSHEET 20-4
Assessing Your Retirement Income

Source	Current Value	Projected Value at Retirement
	$	$
	$	$
	$	$
	$	$
	$	$
	$	$
	$	$
Total projected income:	$	$
Months needed: (85 – your age) × 12 =		
Monthly income: Total projected income ÷ months needed =		

WORKSHEET 20-5

Ideas for Reducing Your Retirement Expenses

Expense	Idea for Reducing or Eliminating	Potential Monthly Savings
		$
		$
		$
		$
		$
		$
		$
		$
		$
		$
		$

Creating a Fifty-Plus Budget

With so many opportunities—from helping your children, grandchildren, and parents to starting a new business or going back to school to ensuring you have enough income in your retirement—you may need to review and rework your budget several times before you can find a way to pay for all of your over-fifty plans. Use **WORKSHEET 20-6** to get you started.

If you don't have enough retirement income to quit working completely at the age you hope to retire, consider looking for a career that you'd enjoy pursuing part time for the next ten or twenty years. You may be able to make enough so that you don't have to tap your retirement funds until much later in life—and you'll have fun.

WORKSHEET 20-6

A Fifty-Plus Budget

Monthly Expense	Amount	Ways to Reduce/Eliminate	New Amount
Groceries and household items	$		$
Contributions	$		$
Savings	$		$
Rent on furniture or appliances	$		$
Entertainment/babysitting	$		$
Eating out	$		$
Rent or mortgage	$		$
Car payment or lease	$		$
Electric bill (average)	$		$
Gas bill (average)	$		$
Water bill	$		$
Sewer bill	$		$
Trash pick-up bill	$		$
Cable/DSL/satellite bill	$		$
Telephone bill	$		$
Cell-phone bill	$		$
Bank charges	$		$
Haircuts/manicures/pedicures	$		$
Home equity loan	$		$
Other loan	$		$
Credit card or store-charge bill	$		$
Credit card or store-charge bill	$		$
Credit card or store-charge bill	$		$
Credit card or store-charge bill	$		$
Credit card or store-charge bill	$		$
Credit card or store-charge bill	$		$

WORKSHEET 20-6

A Fifty-Plus Budget (*continued*)

Monthly Expense	Amount	Ways to Reduce/Eliminate	New Amount
Child support or alimony	$		$
Car maintenance	$		$
House maintenance	$		$
Auto insurance	$		$
Property taxes	$		$
Gifts	$		$
Events to attend	$		$
Clothing and shoes	$		$
Home insurance	$		$
Vehicle registration	$		$
Vacation	$		$
Club membership	$		$
Other:	$		$
Other:	$		$
TOTAL:	$		$

Chapter 21

Saving for Retirement

This chapter gets you started thinking about saving for retirement, but because of space constraints, it only scratches the surface. After reviewing this chapter, dig deeper by reading books that are devoted to the topic of retirement planning, take seminars on the subject, and/or meet with a financial planner.

Figuring Out How Much You'll Need

This is the million-dollar question: How much money will you need in retirement? Unfortunately, there is no set answer. How much you'll need depends on your expenses during your retirement years. If, for example, you will no longer have a house payment or rent in retirement, you may be able to live on a lot less than if you continue to make those payments. On the other hand, if you live in an older house in retirement, you may also encounter more repairs than someone in a new condo.

Use **WORKSHEET 21-1** as a way to begin to determine what your expenses will be during your retirement years. Think of how you live your life now, what will likely change in retirement, and what will be paid off before you retire. (Hint: Don't worry so much about what the actual costs might be down the road; just write in what those costs would be in today's dollars.

WORKSHEET 21-1
Retirement Expenses

Monthly Expense	Amount
Groceries and household items	$
Contributions	$
Savings	$
Rent on furniture or appliances	$
Entertainment	$
Eating out	$
Rent or mortgage	$
Car payment or lease	$
Electric bill (average)	$
Gas bill (average)	$
Sewer bill	$
Water bill	$
Trash pick-up bill	$

WORKSHEET 21-1

Retirement Expenses

Monthly Expense	Amount
Cable/DSL/satellite bill	$
Telephone bill	$
Cell-phone bill	$
Bank charges	$
Haircuts/manicures/pedicures	$
Home equity loan	$
Other loan	$
Credit card or store-charge bill	$
Credit card or store-charge bill	$
Credit card or store-charge bill	$
Credit card or store-charge bill	$
Child support or alimony	$
Car maintenance	$
House maintenance	$
Auto insurance	$
Property taxes	$
Gifts	$
Events to attend	$
Clothing and shoes	$
Home insurance	$
Vehicle registration	$
Vacation	$
Club membership	$
Club membership	$
Other:	$
Total:	$

No one has the ability to look into a crystal ball and know exactly what your expenses will be. The best you can do is estimate, make adjustments, estimate a little more closely, make more adjustments, and on and on!

Finding Ways to Set Money Aside Now

The main reason people put off saving for retirement is that they think they have plenty of time to do that later. The second most popular reason for putting it off is that most people don't know how to come up with money to put into savings. If you've read any of the chapters in the first third of this book, though, you can probably come up with a variety of ways to find $50, $100, or $200 a month for retirement savings. Use **WORKSHEET 21-2** to brainstorm ideas, and review the following sections for some creative ways to save more for retirement.

WORKSHEET 21-2
Ideas for Reducing Your Current Expenses

Expense	Idea for Reducing or Eliminating	Potential Monthly Savings
		$
		$
		$
		$
		$
		$
		$

Stop Eating Out

If you eat take-out twice a week, and you pay $12 for a meal that you could make for $3.50 at home, you could put about $72 a month into your retirement savings. Over twenty years at 5 percent, that's $33,266.94.

Cut Your Clothing and Shoe Budget in Half

If you spend $1,000 per year on clothing and shoes, can you cut that amount in half and put $500 a year ($42 per month) into a retirement account? Thirty years of that at 6 percent, and you'll have $42,189.63 to retire on.

Move to a Smaller House

If you're currently living with two other people in 2,400 square feet, could you move to a house with 1,800 square feet and still be comfortable? If so, your mortgage payments might go down by anywhere from $300 to $1,000 per month, money that you could put into a retirement fund. In just fifteen years at 6 percent, a $600-per-month savings will equal a whopping $157,382.85.

Drive Your Car Twice as Long

If you currently get a new car every three years, pay it off, and get another new one, try something different: Pay off your car in three years but drive it for six. Put the amount of your car payment into a retirement account for the second three years. You'll only contribute to your retirement account three years out of every six, but you'll have found a creative way to save.

FACT

Another way to get more money for retirement is to refinance your mortgage when interest rates decline. For the cost of closing the loan, you might be able to find an extra $50–$150 per month for your retirement savings. Just don't increase the length of the loan, though or you'll sacrifice your long-term financial health.

Start a Part-Time Business

Instead of looking only at potential expenses to cut, consider working a few extra hours per week, perhaps at your own business, and putting that income toward your retirement savings. Chapter 11 has some tips on how to earn a bit more money than you're making now.

Looking at Tax-Deferred Ways to Save

When most people think of retirement and the government at the same time, they think of Social Security, the government program that collects money from you throughout your working life and gives it back to you, one month at a time, during your retirement years.

If you're nearing retirement, you can probably count on quite a bit of Social Security income for your retirement. If you haven't already, you will soon receive a statement that explains how much you'll receive each month, based on exactly what age you retire. You can also contact the Social Security office at *www.ssa.gov* or 800-772-1213.

If you're forty or younger, however, there's isn't much chance that Social Security will fully fund your retirement. That's because instead of taking income from you, investing that income, charging a small administrative fee, and then paying you benefits from the investment, as you may have expected the federal government to do, the system actually works quite differently. The money you paid in isn't there anymore: What you paid in ten years ago was used to pay benefits to other people ten years ago; what you paid in last week was used to pay benefits to other people last week. And that worked pretty well when the largest generation in American history (the baby boomers) were working, but as they near retirement, the government will probably not be able to collect enough in Social Security income to offset the benefits being paid to boomers.

ALERT!

If you're forty or younger, don't count on Social Security to be a part of your retirement package. The money may not be available when it's time for you to draw out the earnings you put in. If it is, that'll be a bonus!

As a result, the government has taken two steps: Increasing the age at which you can begin to draw Social Security benefits; and encouraging you to invest more money in your own retirement accounts to use when you retire. The following sections give you some examples of how they hope to encourage you to do that.

As you investigate all of your options, use **WORKSHEET 21-3** to keep track of what's available to you and how much you're legally allowed to contribute.

WORKSHEET 21-3
Possible Retirement Savings

Type of Account	Possible Contribution	Employer Matching Amount
	$	$
	$	$
	$	$
	$	$
	$	$
	$	$
	$	$
	$	$

Traditional IRA

An individual retirement account (IRA) is a voluntary retirement savings plan. Up to certain limits, you can contribute to an IRA every year and deduct the amount of your contribution from your federal income taxes. Starting at age fifty-nine and a half, you can withdraw funds from your IRA each month. At that time, the money you withdraw is taxed, but because you'll probably be at a lower tax level, you'll still save tax dollars. Withdrawing the money before age fifty-nine and a half results in substantial penalties. In addition, you must begin receiving disbursements from your traditional IRA at age seventy and a half.

FACT

You can make an IRA contribution as late as the day your taxes are due (usually April 15) and still credit your IRA contribution to the previous year's taxes.

As long as you're making money doing something, in 2008 you can deposit $5,000 into a traditional IRA, and that number will likely gradually go up, as it has for the last decade. However, if your income exceeds a certain level, you may not be eligible to take the tax deduction. Consult IRS documents (or visit the IRS Web site at *www.irs.gov*) to determine those income levels for this year. You may also be limited in traditional IRA contributions if your company sponsors a retirement plan for you, even if you don't participate.

Roth IRA

A Roth IRA is a variation of a traditional IRA, but the tax benefits of the plans are in total opposition. With a Roth IRA, instead of getting a tax deduction for your contribution now and paying tax on the amount distributed to you in retirement, you get no tax deduction now, but you pay no tax on the money distributed to you later. Like a traditional IRA, you can contribute $5,000 per year in 2008.

Also like a traditional IRA, however, you can't contribute if you earn too much money ($110,000 for single incomes; $160,000 for joint incomes), and if you earn $95,000–$110,000 for singles ($150,000 and $160,000 for joint filers), the amount you can contribute is less than the full allowable amount.

A Roth IRA does have a couple of benefits over traditional IRAs, though. One is that you can continue to contribute as long as you'd like and do not have to begin taking distributions at age seventy and a half. The other is that you can contribute to a Roth IRA even if your company sponsors a retirement plan.

SEP-IRA

A Simplified Employee Pension (SEP) IRA works like a traditional IRA, but it's set up by an employer for its employees (including by you, if you're self-employed). As long as the employer does not offer another retirement plan, the employer can contribute up to 20 percent of your income (up to $45,000) into the SEP-IRA every year. You can take the account with you when leaving the company to take another job. All of the money contributed comes from your income, but it's not taxed until you receive it during your retirement years.

ALERT!

Looking for a safe way to invest for your retirement? Look into Treasury Inflation-Protected Securities (TIPS), which currently pay around 2.5 percent; plus, they're adjusted for inflation. Although you'll pay tax on the interest if you use them for anything other than retirement, you can buy them for your tax-deferred retirement account(s).

Letting Your Employer Help You

For most of the twentieth century, companies paid the retirement incomes of their long-term employees, so the employees didn't have to worry about saving for their retirement years. How times have changed in the twenty-first century! Most employees do not stay with companies long enough to be considered long term, and most companies do not provide any of their own money to fund retirement accounts. There are a few exceptions, however, discussed in the following sections.

Pension Plan

Your company places money into a retirement account (the amount contributed on your behalf depends on your income, age, and years of service), manages that account, and pays benefits to you from that account when you retire. When you receive distributions from a pension plan (either monthly, annually, or in a lump-sum payment), you're taxed on the income.

Profit Sharing/401(k)/403(b)/457

In this type of plan, your company contributes money, tax free, into an individual account on your behalf based on how much you ask to have contributed (the IRS sets limits, but they're too detailed to include here). Some companies match all or part of these contributions, making your potential annual contribution quite high. Distributions at retirement are taxed. 401(k) plans are used at for-profit companies; 403(b) plans are used at religious, educational, and charitable organizations; 457 plans are used for employees of state and local governments.

SIMPLE-IRA

A Savings Incentive Match Plan for Employees (SIMPLE) IRA is similar to a traditional IRA and a SEP-IRA. A SIMPLE-IRA is set up by a business with fewer than 100 employees (including yours, if you own a small business). Contribution limits to a SIMPLE-IRA are currently over $10,000 and increase each year.

The employer then matches a portion of your contribution—usually a dollar-for-dollar match—for up to 3 percent of your income.

Take advantage of any employer-matching plans, because the employer is offering you free money for retirement. If you can contribute to only one type of retirement account and you have an employer-matching plan at your company, participate in it up to its limits!

Employee Stock Ownership Plan

An Employee Stock Ownership Plan (ESOP) is a retirement account made up mostly of company stock paid for by your employer and, potentially, added to with purchases of company stock that you make. ESOPs can be difficult to take with you if you leave the company, but they can often be transferred into company stock or cash.

Keep in mind that your ESOP is worth only what your company's stock is worth. If you have any doubts about whether your company will still be in business when you retire, don't count on the money from your ESOP as retirement income.

Other Plans

Several dozen other types of employer-contribution plans exist, but many are no longer in existence. For a complete list, visit the Motley Fool's Foolish Retirement Plan Primer at *www.fool.com/Retirement/RetirementPlanPrimer.htm*. You can also visit your local library and ask for help in researching employer-contribution plans.

To find out what your company has to offer, visit the human resources department and ask questions about what's available. You won't have to commit to a plan at that point, but you can use the information to see how much you can save for your retirement with a contribution that's automatically withdrawn from your paycheck.

Investing on Your Own

In addition to putting away retirement savings in tax-deferred or company-sponsored plans, you can always save and invest on your own. Remember, however, that you should first take advantage of any free money your employer might be offering in retirement-matching plans, then take advantage of tax-deferred retirement plans, and only as a third choice begin a simple savings account or a more complex investment portfolio for your retirement income.

Saving money in a savings account is quite simple and doesn't require any particular knowledge or skill. You may want to periodically shift your savings to a long-term CD or to savings bonds to earn a higher interest rate.

Once you begin investing, you'll probably want to have an accountant figure your taxes every year. You may owe tax on your earnings, and figuring out exactly how much is a pretty complicated procedure.

Investing, which is significantly more complicated, requires some knowledge of the markets, company documents, and trading rules. If you're interested in learning more about investing, do it. If you're conservative in your investments and take time to read all the available financial documents on companies in which you're investing, the risk is far smaller than most people believe. If you have no interest in doing this, hire a stockbroker or financial consultant to invest for you.

Starting Young

The absolute best way to save for retirement is to start young. If you start saving $100 per month when you're twenty-five, and you invest that in a mutual fund or other stock-related fund that sometimes earns 18-percent interest and sometimes loses money, averaging 8 percent over the next forty years, you'll have $351,428.13 for retirement. To get the same amount of retirement savings if you start at age forty, you'll have to put away about $367 per month. Use the Savings Growth Projector Calculator at *www.finaid.org* to run these numbers for yourself.

Making Up for Lost Time

Regardless of how old you are, you can still save some money for your retirement, thanks to the government's catch-up provision, which allows you to save more money in a retirement account when you're over fifty than when you were younger. You may also be able to use the equity you've built up in your house to fund part of your retirement. The following two sections share some details about each option.

Using the Catch-Up Provision

If you're over fifty, you're allowed to put away more tax-free income per year than your younger counterparts. For example, while the standard contribution to both traditional and Roth IRAs is $5,000 per year (subject to income limits, of course), anyone over fifty can contribute $1,000 more than that. Your company's 401(k) plan has similar provisions, allowing you to contribute more than younger workers. This is called a catch-up provision, and it's meant specifically for people who started saving for retirement later in life.

Using Your House to Help You Retire

If you haven't made many provisions for your retirement and can't seem to find the money to do so, you may be able to tap the value of your house for your retirement. Suppose you're forty-five years old and have fifteen years left to pay on your house. You bought the house fifteen years ago, and home prices have risen significantly since then. Your house is worth $240,000 now and will likely be worth over $450,000 when you turn sixty and the house is paid off.

Rather than staying in the house during retirement, you can sell it and move to a smaller house or condominium that costs far less. If you can sell your house for $450,000 and buy a condo at that time for $300,000 or $350,000, you'll have $100,000 to $150,000 to add to your retirement account.

ESSENTIAL

If mortgage interest rates drop to one point or lower than the rate on your mortgage, consider refinancing. You may be able to get a shorter loan length (say, fifteen years instead of thirty) for the same monthly payments. This can enhance your ability to use your house as part of your retirement plan.

On the other hand, you can stay in the house and get a reverse mortgage on it as soon as you begin needing income (say, when you turn sixty-five or seventy). Essentially, a bank buys the house back from you, except that you continue to own it and live in it. You must be at least sixty-two and own the house free and clear. The bank then either sends you monthly payments or gives you a lump sum. You'll pay a fee for this service because if you live longer than the bank thinks you're going to live, they may actually lose money on the deal. Still, many lenders offer this option.

Chapter 22
Staying Motivated

When you have financial goals, especially long-term ones, that force you to cut your expenses to the bone and, potentially, work a second job, you may have trouble staying motivated at times. This chapter is meant to encourage and inspire you through those tough times.

Sticking with Your Budget Through Thick and Thin

The best way to stay motivated when you're weary from saving every spare dime is to have already decided from the get-go that you're going to stick to your budget no matter what. This is called discipline—deciding that, no matter who tries to influence you, you're going to reach your financial goals and not let anything or anyone get you off track.

When you're establishing financial goals, don't use words or phrases like "try," "would like to," or "might." State your goals as strongly as you can: "I will pay off my credit card debt by September of next year," instead of "I'll try to pay off my credit cards" or "I'd like to pay off my credit cards." The primary difference is in the attitude you take about your ability to control your finances.

Unfortunately, discipline isn't easy, and if you don't make a full commitment to your budget when you establish it, you may find yourself opting for small pleasures now that get you further into debt, put you back in debt after you've gotten out, or simply delay reaching your financial goals for that many more months or years. If that's the case, decide now—right this very minute—that you're going to stick to your budget no matter what.

Making Motivational Signs

To stay motivated to stick to your budget, make inspirational signs for yourself and put them in places around your home where you're likely to see them, and in your wallet! Here are some examples:

- I'm going back to school next year.
- I will retire at age fifty-five.

- I am buying a house next spring.
- I will be out of debt by the last day of June.
- I'm buying my granddaughter a bike for her birthday.

Your signs can say anything you want, as long as they're meaningful to you and address your most important financial goals. Place large ones on your refrigerator and on your bedroom nightstand; tape smaller ones to your coffeemaker and bathroom mirror. Place one in your wallet, wrapped around your credit card, debit card, or cash. If you tend to shop from catalogs, place one on your phone. If Internet shopping is your downfall, place one of your signs on your computer. These signs should help you stick to your budget and reach your long-term financial goals.

Having too many of these signs won't motivate you—they'll just make you laugh! If you find yourself needing signs everywhere to keep you motivated, try making a sign that says, "I will stop making these signs!" That should be fun for a few days.

If You Blow Your Budget—Getting Back on Track

Suppose you get off track. You get so tired of living like a monk that you put your credit card back in your wallet, drive to your local shopping mall, and under the guise of "it's on sale," buy a few hundred dollars worth of clothes or electronic equipment. Yet you don't have any way to pay for these purchases, except by taking money out of savings, or worse, by paying your credit card company until it's paid off.

If this happens, stay calm. Nobody's perfect, and after you've come this far on your financial journey, this small setback won't kill you! You can, however, take some steps toward minimizing the effects of your shopping spree:

1. Don't remove tags or open boxes from any purchases for one week.
2. One week after you buy any item, see how you feel about returning it for a refund.
3. If a refund isn't possible, either because the store won't accept returned merchandise or because you ripped the tags off the minute you got home, see whether a friend or relative wants to buy the item from you at full price.
4. If a refund or sale isn't possible, revisit your budget to see how you can pay for this item.

You may find that, in order to pay for your splurge, you have to cut back your expenses even further than before or get a part-time job to pay off the debt. If that's the case, do it. Whatever you do, don't go back into debt because of one small slipup.

QUESTION?

Is there a law that makes stores accept returns?
Absolutely not. Every business is allowed to set its own return policies, but if a store doesn't accept returns, or if they give only a store credit, they must tell you this on the receipt, in person, or on visible signs.

Finding Sneaky Ways to Spend Money

Finding ways to spend money on yourself now and then is critical to your continuing ability to save and spend wisely. The problem is that treating yourself is usually expensive and can blow your budget. This section gives you some ideas on how you can celebrate your budgeted life in easy and inexpensive ways.

Make a List of Free Activities

Sit down and make a list of free activities that you enjoy. These activities might include watching a certain television program, visiting a nearby park, playing in the backyard with your dog, sitting on your porch reading a library book, attending a free concert, taking a bath, and so on.

When you have your list ready, treat yourself to one of these activities every time you meet a financial milestone, even if it's just writing out a check to your credit card company for more than the minimum amount due. Because you'll look forward to these free activities, you'll also be motivated to stick to even the most tiresome budget.

Give Yourself Five Dollars to Splurge

Giving yourself such a small amount of money to splurge when you meet your financial goals may not seem very motivating, but you might be amazed at what you can do with $5. You can see a matinee movie; eat lunch at a fast-food restaurant; rent a DVD and buy two chocolate bars; purchase a new pair of socks; buy a paperback book; or get a new coffee or tea mug. The point isn't *what* you do, as much as *that* you do it. With your $5 in hand, you can focus on spending it on the perfect thing for you. And that will tide you over until the next time you can splurge with $5 again.

If your budget allows for a smaller or larger amount than $5 as periodic splurging money, make a list of what you can get with $1 or $10. You can be just as creative with any amount of money.

Reinvigorate Something You Already Own

When you're bogged down with paying off your debts and feel like you need to have something new in your life, consider sprucing up something you already own and giving it to yourself—even wrapping it up as a present! One simple way to do this is to go through your closet and find an article of clothing that you like but haven't worn in a while. Giving it to yourself again will help it seem like a fresh purchase. If it makes your wardrobe seem newer and fresher, you may feel as though you've been treated to something new.

Pretend to Spend

If you have catalogs around or have access to the Internet or are willing to take a window-shopping trip to the mall, you can satisfy some of your urge to spend by making a detailed list of what you would spend money on if you could. Just imagine that you won the lottery, and start considering what you would buy: A new car? A new wardrobe? A new house? Whatever it would be, decide exactly what you would buy—but then don't buy it.

Warning: If you're not very disciplined, don't try this activity. It might be really fun deciding what to buy, looking at cars, and filling out order forms, but under no circumstances can you actually purchase these items! If you think you might be tempted, choose one of the other ideas in this chapter.

When you're faced with the reality of sticking to a strict budget, you may want to cancel all of the catalogs that come to your house. Just call the 800 numbers and ask that your name be removed from their mailing lists. This may reduce your temptation to spend.

Imagine Yourself Reaching Your Goals

One sure way to treat yourself for free is to find a comfortable spot to sit, and then imagine yourself reaching your financial goals. Visualize yourself sitting in your new house, watching your child's college graduation, being treated to a retirement party at whatever age you decide on, and so on. Do this every time your strict budget gets you down.

Building a Support Network

To stay disciplined and motivated to meet your financial goals, enlist the help of one or two close friends. Begin by summarizing your current financial situation and goals (don't be too specific, just give the highlights), then ask your friend whether you can call him or her for support from time to time. Just be sure that this is a friend who will help you stick to the plan, not one who will tempt you to abandon your budget and get further away from your financial goals. Choose someone whose spending and saving habits you admire.

If you have a friend who has plenty of money to spend, don't be jealous! Instead, accept that you're in two different places in your lives. You may even be able to spend vicariously through your friend, going along on shopping trips. Just be sure to leave your credit and debit cards behind!

You may also want to create a financial support group made up of friends, family members, neighbors, coworkers, and so on. Members commit to creating a budget and share their financial goals with the group, which meets periodically. During meetings, group members share their frustrations and disappointments, but also their successes. If you can find even a small group of like-minded budgeters, you can create a financial support group.

Reviewing Your Budget Periodically

If your budget no longer fits your situation or moves you toward your financial goals, you won't be motivated to stick to it. Ultimately, for a budget to be successful, it has to be relevant.

In all probability, after you created your first budget, you gave a deep sigh of relief and figured you'd never have to do that again. Unfortunately, you not only have to continue to update your budget, you have to do it fairly often. The following sections describe the situations that usually call for revising your budget.

Whenever Your Income Rises or Falls Considerably

Every time you get a raise, even a small one, you need to revisit your budget. That small raise might be the difference between paying off your credit cards in two years instead of three, but that can't happen if you fritter it away.

If your income should drop, you also need to revisit your budget right away. Even a small drop in income can change your entire financial picture.

Whenever Your Expenses Rise or Fall Considerably

Whenever your expenses change, you'll need a new budget. If, for example, you refinance your house from a thirty-year mortgage to a fifteen-year loan, your monthly payments may go up somewhat. This may mean you have to cut back in other areas to afford the new payment.

Whenever Your Family Changes Size

Whether by birth, death, or a parent or other family member coming to live with you, changes in your family's size will result in changes in your expenses, and these changes mean that you need a new budget. A budget tells you how your financial picture will be affected by your income and expenses, and a new family member may have a significant impact on your ability to meet your financial goals. On the other hand, when your youngest leaves the house, you may find that you have significantly more money to spend or save. Revisiting your budget can help you see where to put this newfound money. (Chapter 20 guides you through empty-nest syndrome.)

Whenever You Receive an Inheritance or Other Windfall

Your first reaction at receiving any lump sum of money may be to spend, spend, spend. All that pent-up consumerism may be tempted to run wild with this influx of cash.

Suppose one of your financial goals is to save enough for a 20-percent down payment on a house, and that's going to cost you about $40,000. For the last year, you've been sticking to your budget and have over $6,000 saved. Now you receive $30,000 from a rich uncle who recently passed away. You think of getting new golf clubs or new furniture, right? Not so fast! Revisit that budget, and you'll find that if you put your inheritance into savings, you're now just $4,000 away from buying that new house. And at the rate you've been saving, you can save that in eight months.

If you use your windfall wisely, you could reach some of your financial goals years, maybe even decades, sooner! But if you spend the money foolishly, you may regret it for years or decades.

Whenever Your Goals Shift

Don't be surprised if your goals change quite a bit as time goes on. One great example of this is how meaningless retirement savings seems to twenty-somethings. In fact, some forty-year-olds are still too far from retirement to care. But the fact is, as your friends and coworkers begin to retire, saving for your own retirement will likely become your number-one financial goal, and you'll attack it with a vengeance.

Your other goals may change, too. Some, like paying off credit cards or buying a house, will disappear because you've reached them. Others, like retiring at age forty or buying a beach house, may simply disappear because you can't cut your expenses or raise your income enough to ever meet those goals. Still others, like paying 100 percent of your kids' college costs, may be replaced with more practical goals, like paying 50 or 75 percent of those costs.

Your goals may begin to shift because of the reality that a budget brings to your financial life. If that's the case, accept that certain goals simply aren't possible, and move forward with the ones that are. But other goals may change for other reasons, and you'll need to pull out your budget to see how these new goals can fit into your financial plan. Perhaps, for example, you had originally thought you would retire at age fifty, but now have a new goal: To retire from your current job at age fifty and start a new business that you'll work at part time until you turn sixty-five. That new goal will have its own expenses and timelines that need to be incorporated into a new budget.

Appendix A

Debt-Restructuring Resources

Looking for assistance in restructuring your debt? The nonprofit organizations listed here can intervene with your creditors on your behalf, lowering your interest rates and allowing you to make a single payment each month to pay off your debt, usually in five years or so.

The credit-counseling agencies listed in this appendix make up some of the largest in the United States. That does not imply, however, that they're any better than an agency in your local area—and yours may be much more personalized and convenient. To find an agency in your area, look under Credit Counseling in your Yellow Pages. To use the Internet, search using the words "credit counseling" and the name of your city or area.

Don't forget to ask whether the credit-counseling agency you're thinking of using is a nonprofit organization. If it isn't, go elsewhere!

American Family Credit Counseling, Inc.

American Family Credit Counseling offers credit counseling, budgeting, and debt-management plans that can help you become debt-free. Counselors help you lower your interest rates, lower your payments, and still pay off the entire amounts in three to five years.

877-FOR-DEBT

www.fordebt.org

Association of Independent Consumer Credit Counseling Agencies (AICCCA)

The AICCCA Web site provides a link to finding a counseling agency in your area. (They do not offer a toll-free phone number.) This agency was created by credit counselors and exists to ensure that all credit counselors (not just member agencies) maintain professional standards. If you want to know whether a particular agency is on the level, check out AICCCA's Web site.

www.aiccca.org

Better Business Bureau (BBB)

The Better Business Bureau offers advice on choosing a credit-counseling agency. You can also call your local BBB at the number in your phone book. The BBB was set up as a nonprofit organization that tracks the way companies do business. They log complaints from consumers (including yours, if you have a business), so that when you call and ask about a particular company's reputation, the BBB can tell you how many and what sort of complaints the company has received. The BBB exists in the vast majority of areas in the United States and is one of the most respected agencies in the country.

www.bbb.org/alerts/article.asp?ID=613

Consumer Credit Counseling Services (CCCS)

Consumer Credit Counseling Services and its parent company, Money Management International, together make up the largest credit-counseling agency in the United States. The Web site offers tools, articles, and advice, and also allows you to receive their counseling services online. You can also call to receive credit counseling over the phone.
866-889-9347
www.moneymanagement.org

The Council on Accreditation of Services for Families and Children (COA)

The COA serves as an advocate for families and children. When searching for a credit-counseling agency, look for the COA seal of accreditation, which indicates that an agency meets the highest industry standards. You can also get a list of accredited organizations by checking COA's Web site—the site is easy to use and simply lists the organizations by state. You can also call toll-free.
866-262-8088
www.coanet.org

Federal Trade Commission (FTC)

The Federal Trade Commission provides helpful information on choosing a credit-counseling agency. Keep in mind that the FTC is pretty unbiased. Although they'd like you to have less debt because it keeps the economy healthier, they also want to nab the unscrupulous credit counselors who have set up shop. Bottom line: You can trust the FTC.
877-FTC-HELP
www.ftc.gov/bcp/conline/pubs/credit/fiscal.shtm

National Foundation for Credit Counseling (NFCC)

The NFCC is the nation's oldest nonprofit network of credit counselors, offering more than 1,300 offices across the United States. They recommend that you look for the NFCC seal before choosing a credit-counseling agency. The seal signifies high standards, trained counselors, and free or low-cost services. For a referral to a credit-counseling agency in your area, call or visit their Web site.
800-388-2227
www.nfcc.org

Appendix B

Budgeting Web Sites and Online Tools

Web sites devoted to budgeting are few and far between, but the Web sites listed here provide some unique features that you may not be able to find in a book or other publication. While these sites are current as of this book's printing, be prepared for them to change at any time.

About.com: Credit and Debt Management

At any given time, on the credit and debt management site at About.com, you'll find over a dozen useful tips, articles, and online tools.
http://credit.about.com/cs/budgeting

Bankrate.com

Bankrate's site is a veritable treasure trove of financial advice. Tips include everything from protecting your identity to getting a car loan to personal finance blogs. If you have questions, chances are this site will give you answers.
www.bankrate.com

Better Budgeting

This e-zine, albeit not strong on design or organization, contains featured articles and columns that pertain mostly to families with children, but many of the tips apply to just about anyone. On any given day, it may cover topics as wide-ranging as home schooling, job hunting, and the price of Treasury bills.
www.betterbudgeting.com

The Dollar Stretcher

This isn't the fanciest or prettiest site on the Internet, but it does offer a plethora of ideas for cutting costs and stretching your dollar.
www.stretcher.com

FinCalc.com

If you want to visit one site that has nearly every financial calculator imaginable, take a look at this site. There you'll find calculators that help you figure how long paying off your credit cards will take, how much retirement income you can accumulate, what you'll save by refinancing your house, how much you can save in your child's college fund, and more.
www.fincalc.com

HSH Associates

At this site, you'll find just about anything you want to know about mortgages. From current mortgage rates to advice on removing your PMI, this site gives you good information if you're thinking about getting a new (or first) mortgage, refinancing, or getting a home equity loan.
www.hsh.com

Kiplinger's

The guru of financial publishers, Kiplinger's useful budgeting Web site includes calculators and other tools for determining your financial worth and establishing a budget. You'll find everything from establishing your current financial position to establishing financial goals to staying out of financial traps. This is a good, all-around budgeting site.
www.kiplinger.com

Marketplace

Many public radio stations feature Marketplace each weekday evening, a broad-based program covering the economy, the business world, and personal finance. The Marketplace Web site is a useful extension of that show, sharing tips on home buying, investing, and so on.
http://marketplace.publicradio.org

Nolo

The Nolo site covers all sorts of legal topics in plain English, and the section on Credit Repair & Debts may answer a lot of your questions about getting rid of collection agencies, restoring your credit, paying off debt (including student loans), and filing for bankruptcy protection. In addition, you'll find up-to-date law changes and additions regarding debt management. This site also offers some useful financial calculators and download-able worksheets.
www.nolo.com

SavingAdvice.com

This site is all about helping you save money. Frequently updated, the site features excellent tips on saving money day to day, which frees up money to help you reach your financial goals.
www.savingadvice.com

SmartMoney.com

SmartMoney's personal-finance page is a smorgasbord of budgeting ideas and tools. Perhaps the best feature is SmartMoney's incredibly cool mortgage calculator, which tells you what your monthly payments will be for a house, the difference between fifteen- and thirty-year mortgages, and more. Click on the Real Estate section on the left-hand side of the screen and click on The Mortgage Calculator. It also offers up-to-date information on college savings, taxes, retirement planning, investment tools, and so on.
www.smartmoney.com/pf

Index

THE EVERYTHING SERIES!

BUSINESS & PERSONAL FINANCE

Everything® Accounting Book
Everything® Budgeting Book, 2nd Ed.
Everything® Business Planning Book
Everything® Coaching and Mentoring Book, 2nd Ed.
Everything® Fundraising Book
Everything® Get Out of Debt Book
Everything® Grant Writing Book, 2nd Ed.
Everything® Guide to Buying Foreclosures
Everything® Guide to Mortgages
Everything® Guide to Personal Finance for Single Mothers
Everything® Home-Based Business Book, 2nd Ed.
Everything® Homebuying Book, 2nd Ed.
Everything® Homeselling Book, 2nd Ed.
Everything® Human Resource Management Book
Everything® Improve Your Credit Book
Everything® Investing Book, 2nd Ed.
Everything® Landlording Book
Everything® Leadership Book, 2nd Ed.
Everything® Managing People Book, 2nd Ed.
Everything® Negotiating Book
Everything® Online Auctions Book
Everything® Online Business Book
Everything® Personal Finance Book
Everything® Personal Finance in Your 20s & 30s Book, 2nd Ed.
Everything® Project Management Book, 2nd Ed.
Everything® Real Estate Investing Book
Everything® Retirement Planning Book
Everything® Robert's Rules Book, $7.95
Everything® Selling Book
Everything® Start Your Own Business Book, 2nd Ed.
Everything® Wills & Estate Planning Book

COOKING

Everything® Barbecue Cookbook
Everything® Bartender's Book, 2nd Ed., $9.95
Everything® Calorie Counting Cookbook
Everything® Cheese Book
Everything® Chinese Cookbook
Everything® Classic Recipes Book
Everything® Cocktail Parties & Drinks Book
Everything® College Cookbook
Everything® Cooking for Baby and Toddler Book
Everything® Cooking for Two Cookbook
Everything® Diabetes Cookbook
Everything® Easy Gourmet Cookbook
Everything® Fondue Cookbook
Everything® Fondue Party Book
Everything® Gluten-Free Cookbook
Everything® Glycemic Index Cookbook
Everything® Grilling Cookbook
Everything® Healthy Meals in Minutes Cookbook
Everything® Holiday Cookbook
Everything® Indian Cookbook
Everything® Italian Cookbook

Everything® Lactose-Free Cookbook
Everything® Low-Carb Cookbook
Everything® Low-Cholesterol Cookbook
Everything® Low-Fat High-Flavor Cookbook
Everything® Low-Salt Cookbook
Everything® Meals for a Month Cookbook
Everything® Meals on a Budget Cookbook
Everything® Mediterranean Cookbook
Everything® Mexican Cookbook
Everything® No Trans Fat Cookbook
Everything® One-Pot Cookbook
Everything® Pizza Cookbook
Everything® Quick and Easy 30-Minute, 5-Ingredient Cookbook
Everything® Quick Meals Cookbook
Everything® Slow Cooker Cookbook
Everything® Slow Cooking for a Crowd Cookbook
Everything® Soup Cookbook
Everything® Stir-Fry Cookbook
Everything® Sugar-Free Cookbook
Everything® Tapas and Small Plates Cookbook
Everything® Tex-Mex Cookbook
Everything® Thai Cookbook
Everything® Vegetarian Cookbook
Everything® Whole-Grain, High-Fiber Cookbook
Everything® Wild Game Cookbook
Everything® Wine Book, 2nd Ed.

GAMES

Everything® 15-Minute Sudoku Book, $9.95
Everything® 30-Minute Sudoku Book, $9.95
Everything® Bible Crosswords Book, $9.95
Everything® Blackjack Strategy Book
Everything® Brain Strain Book, $9.95
Everything® Bridge Book
Everything® Card Games Book
Everything® Card Tricks Book, $9.95
Everything® Casino Gambling Book, 2nd Ed.
Everything® Chess Basics Book
Everything® Craps Strategy Book
Everything® Crossword and Puzzle Book
Everything® Crossword Challenge Book
Everything® Crosswords for the Beach Book, $9.95
Everything® Cryptic Crosswords Book, $9.95
Everything® Cryptograms Book, $9.95
Everything® Easy Crosswords Book
Everything® Easy Kakuro Book, $9.95
Everything® Easy Large-Print Crosswords Book
Everything® Games Book, 2nd Ed.
Everything® Giant Sudoku Book, $9.95
Everything® Giant Word Search Book
Everything® Kakuro Challenge Book, $9.95
Everything® Large-Print Crossword Challenge Book
Everything® Large-Print Crosswords Book
Everything® Lateral Thinking Puzzles Book, $9.95
Everything® Literary Crosswords Book, $9.95
Everything® Mazes Book
Everything® Memory Booster Puzzles Book, $9.95
Everything® Movie Crosswords Book, $9.95

Everything® Music Crosswords Book, $9.95
Everything® Online Poker Book
Everything® Pencil Puzzles Book, $9.95
Everything® Poker Strategy Book
Everything® Pool & Billiards Book
Everything® Puzzles for Commuters Book, $9.95
Everything® Puzzles for Dog Lovers Book, $9.95
Everything® Sports Crosswords Book, $9.95
Everything® Test Your IQ Book, $9.95
Everything® Texas Hold 'Em Book, $9.95
Everything® Travel Crosswords Book, $9.95
Everything® TV Crosswords Book, $9.95
Everything® Word Games Challenge Book
Everything® Word Scramble Book
Everything® Word Search Book

HEALTH

Everything® Alzheimer's Book
Everything® Diabetes Book
Everything® First Aid Book, $9.95
Everything® Health Guide to Adult Bipolar Disorder
Everything® Health Guide to Arthritis
Everything® Health Guide to Controlling Anxiety
Everything® Health Guide to Depression
Everything® Health Guide to Fibromyalgia
Everything® Health Guide to Menopause, 2nd Ed.
Everything® Health Guide to Migraines
Everything® Health Guide to OCD
Everything® Health Guide to PMS
Everything® Health Guide to Postpartum Care
Everything® Health Guide to Thyroid Disease
Everything® Hypnosis Book
Everything® Low Cholesterol Book
Everything® Menopause Book
Everything® Nutrition Book
Everything® Reflexology Book
Everything® Stress Management Book

HISTORY

Everything® American Government Book
Everything® American History Book, 2nd Ed.
Everything® Civil War Book
Everything® Freemasons Book
Everything® Irish History & Heritage Book
Everything® Middle East Book
Everything® World War II Book, 2nd Ed.

HOBBIES

Everything® Candlemaking Book
Everything® Cartooning Book
Everything® Coin Collecting Book
Everything® Digital Photography Book, 2nd Ed.
Everything® Drawing Book
Everything® Family Tree Book, 2nd Ed.
Everything® Knitting Book
Everything® Knots Book
Everything® Photography Book
Everything® Quilting Book

Everything® Sewing Book
Everything® Soapmaking Book, 2nd Ed.
Everything® Woodworking Book

HOME IMPROVEMENT

Everything® Feng Shui Book
Everything® Feng Shui Decluttering Book, $9.95
Everything® Fix-It Book
Everything® Green Living Book
Everything® Home Decorating Book
Everything® Home Storage Solutions Book
Everything® Homebuilding Book
Everything® Organize Your Home Book, 2nd Ed.

KIDS' BOOKS

All titles are $7.95

Everything® Fairy Tales Book, $14.95
Everything® Kids' Animal Puzzle & Activity Book
Everything® Kids' Astronomy Book
Everything® Kids' Baseball Book, 5th Ed.
Everything® Kids' Bible Trivia Book
Everything® Kids' Bugs Book
Everything® Kids' Cars and Trucks Puzzle and Activity Book
Everything® Kids' Christmas Puzzle & Activity Book
Everything® Kids' Connect the Dots
Puzzle and Activity Book
Everything® Kids' Cookbook
Everything® Kids' Crazy Puzzles Book
Everything® Kids' Dinosaurs Book
Everything® Kids' Environment Book
Everything® Kids' Fairies Puzzle and Activity Book
Everything® Kids' First Spanish Puzzle and Activity Book
Everything® Kids' Football Book
Everything® Kids' Gross Cookbook
Everything® Kids' Gross Hidden Pictures Book
Everything® Kids' Gross Jokes Book
Everything® Kids' Gross Mazes Book
Everything® Kids' Gross Puzzle & Activity Book
Everything® Kids' Halloween Puzzle & Activity Book
Everything® Kids' Hidden Pictures Book
Everything® Kids' Horses Book
Everything® Kids' Joke Book
Everything® Kids' Knock Knock Book
Everything® Kids' Learning French Book
Everything® Kids' Learning Spanish Book
Everything® Kids' Magical Science Experiments Book
Everything® Kids' Math Puzzles Book
Everything® Kids' Mazes Book
Everything® Kids' Money Book
Everything® Kids' Nature Book
Everything® Kids' Pirates Puzzle and Activity Book
Everything® Kids' Presidents Book
Everything® Kids' Princess Puzzle and Activity Book
Everything® Kids' Puzzle Book
Everything® Kids' Racecars Puzzle and Activity Book
Everything® Kids' Riddles & Brain Teasers Book
Everything® Kids' Science Experiments Book
Everything® Kids' Sharks Book
Everything® Kids' Soccer Book
Everything® Kids' Spies Puzzle and Activity Book
Everything® Kids' States Book
Everything® Kids' Travel Activity Book
Everything® Kids' Word Search Puzzle and Activity Book

LANGUAGE

Everything® Conversational Japanese Book with CD, $19.95
Everything® French Grammar Book
Everything® French Phrase Book, $9.95
Everything® French Verb Book, $9.95
Everything® German Practice Book with CD, $19.95
Everything® Inglés Book
Everything® Intermediate Spanish Book with CD, $19.95
Everything® Italian Practice Book with CD, $19.95
Everything® Learning Brazilian Portuguese Book with CD, $19.95
Everything® Learning French Book with CD, 2nd Ed., $19.95
Everything® Learning German Book
Everything® Learning Italian Book
Everything® Learning Latin Book
Everything® Learning Russian Book with CD, $19.95
Everything® Learning Spanish Book
Everything® Learning Spanish Book with CD, 2nd Ed., $19.95
Everything® Russian Practice Book with CD, $19.95
Everything® Sign Language Book
Everything® Spanish Grammar Book
Everything® Spanish Phrase Book, $9.95
Everything® Spanish Practice Book with CD, $19.95
Everything® Spanish Verb Book, $9.95
Everything® Speaking Mandarin Chinese Book with CD, $19.95

MUSIC

Everything® Bass Guitar Book with CD, $19.95
Everything® Drums Book with CD, $19.95
Everything® Guitar Book with CD, 2nd Ed., $19.95
Everything® Guitar Chords Book with CD, $19.95
Everything® Harmonica Book with CD, $15.95
Everything® Home Recording Book
Everything® Music Theory Book with CD, $19.95
Everything® Reading Music Book with CD, $19.95
Everything® Rock & Blues Guitar Book with CD, $19.95
Everything® Rock & Blues Piano Book with CD, $19.95
Everything® Songwriting Book

NEW AGE

Everything® Astrology Book, 2nd Ed.
Everything® Birthday Personology Book
Everything® Dreams Book, 2nd Ed.
Everything® Love Signs Book, $9.95
Everything® Love Spells Book, $9.95
Everything® Paganism Book
Everything® Palmistry Book
Everything® Psychic Book
Everything® Reiki Book
Everything® Sex Signs Book, $9.95
Everything® Spells & Charms Book, 2nd Ed.
Everything® Tarot Book, 2nd Ed.
Everything® Toltec Wisdom Book
Everything® Wicca & Witchcraft Book, 2nd Ed.

PARENTING

Everything® Baby Names Book, 2nd Ed.
Everything® Baby Shower Book, 2nd Ed.
Everything® Baby Sign Language Book with DVD
Everything® Baby's First Year Book
Everything® Birthing Book

Everything® Breastfeeding Book
Everything® Father-to-Be Book
Everything® Father's First Year Book
Everything® Get Ready for Baby Book, 2nd Ed.
Everything® Get Your Baby to Sleep Book, $9.95
Everything® Getting Pregnant Book
Everything® Guide to Pregnancy Over 35
Everything® Guide to Raising a One-Year-Old
Everything® Guide to Raising a Two-Year-Old
Everything® Guide to Raising Adolescent Boys
Everything® Guide to Raising Adolescent Girls
Everything® Mother's First Year Book
Everything® Parent's Guide to Childhood Illnesses
Everything® Parent's Guide to Children and Divorce
Everything® Parent's Guide to Children with ADD/ADHD
Everything® Parent's Guide to Children with Asperger's Syndrome
Everything® Parent's Guide to Children with Asthma
Everything® Parent's Guide to Children with Autism
Everything® Parent's Guide to Children with Bipolar Disorder
Everything® Parent's Guide to Children with Depression
Everything® Parent's Guide to Children with Dyslexia
Everything® Parent's Guide to Children with Juvenile Diabetes
Everything® Parent's Guide to Positive Discipline
Everything® Parent's Guide to Raising a Successful Child
Everything® Parent's Guide to Raising Boys
Everything® Parent's Guide to Raising Girls
Everything® Parent's Guide to Raising Siblings
Everything® Parent's Guide to Sensory Integration Disorder
Everything® Parent's Guide to Tantrums
Everything® Parent's Guide to the Strong-Willed Child
Everything® Parenting a Teenager Book
Everything® Potty Training Book, $9.95
Everything® Pregnancy Book, 3rd Ed.
Everything® Pregnancy Fitness Book
Everything® Pregnancy Nutrition Book
Everything® Pregnancy Organizer, 2nd Ed., $16.95
Everything® Toddler Activities Book
Everything® Toddler Book
Everything® Tween Book
Everything® Twins, Triplets, and More Book

PETS

Everything® Aquarium Book
Everything® Boxer Book
Everything® Cat Book, 2nd Ed.
Everything® Chihuahua Book
Everything® Cooking for Dogs Book
Everything® Dachshund Book
Everything® Dog Book, 2nd Ed.
Everything® Dog Grooming Book
Everything® Dog Health Book
Everything® Dog Obedience Book
Everything® Dog Owner's Organizer, $16.95
Everything® Dog Training and Tricks Book
Everything® German Shepherd Book
Everything® Golden Retriever Book
Everything® Horse Book
Everything® Horse Care Book
Everything® Horseback Riding Book
Everything® Labrador Retriever Book
Everything® Poodle Book
Everything® Pug Book

Everything® Puppy Book
Everything® Rottweiler Book
Everything® Small Dogs Book
Everything® Tropical Fish Book
Everything® Yorkshire Terrier Book

REFERENCE

Everything® American Presidents Book
Everything® Blogging Book
Everything® Build Your Vocabulary Book, $9.95
Everything® Car Care Book
Everything® Classical Mythology Book
Everything® Da Vinci Book
Everything® Divorce Book
Everything® Einstein Book
Everything® Enneagram Book
Everything® Etiquette Book, 2nd Ed.
Everything® Guide to C. S. Lewis & Narnia
Everything® Guide to Edgar Allan Poe
Everything® Guide to Understanding Philosophy
Everything® Inventions and Patents Book
Everything® Jacqueline Kennedy Onassis Book
Everything® John F. Kennedy Book
Everything® Mafia Book
Everything® Martin Luther King Jr. Book
Everything® Philosophy Book
Everything® Pirates Book
Everything® Private Investigation Book
Everything® Psychology Book
Everything® Public Speaking Book, $9.95
Everything® Shakespeare Book, 2nd Ed.

RELIGION

Everything® Angels Book
Everything® Bible Book
Everything® Bible Study Book with CD, $19.95
Everything® Buddhism Book
Everything® Catholicism Book
Everything® Christianity Book
Everything® Gnostic Gospels Book
Everything® History of the Bible Book
Everything® Jesus Book
Everything® Jewish History & Heritage Book
Everything® Judaism Book
Everything® Kabbalah Book
Everything® Koran Book
Everything® Mary Book
Everything® Mary Magdalene Book
Everything® Prayer Book
Everything® Saints Book, 2nd Ed.
Everything® Torah Book
Everything® Understanding Islam Book
Everything® Women of the Bible Book
Everything® World's Religions Book

SCHOOL & CAREERS

Everything® Career Tests Book
Everything® College Major Test Book
Everything® College Survival Book, 2nd Ed.
Everything® Cover Letter Book, 2nd Ed.
Everything® Filmmaking Book
Everything® Get-a-Job Book, 2nd Ed.
Everything® Guide to Being a Paralegal
Everything® Guide to Being a Personal Trainer
Everything® Guide to Being a Real Estate Agent
Everything® Guide to Being a Sales Rep
Everything® Guide to Being an Event Planner
Everything® Guide to Careers in Health Care
Everything® Guide to Careers in Law Enforcement
Everything® Guide to Government Jobs
Everything® Guide to Starting and Running a Catering
     Business
Everything® Guide to Starting and Running a Restaurant
Everything® Job Interview Book, 2nd Ed.
Everything® New Nurse Book
Everything® New Teacher Book
Everything® Paying for College Book
Everything® Practice Interview Book
Everything® Resume Book, 3rd Ed.
Everything® Study Book

SELF-HELP

Everything® Body Language Book
Everything® Dating Book, 2nd Ed.
Everything® Great Sex Book
Everything® Self-Esteem Book
Everything® Tantric Sex Book

SPORTS & FITNESS

Everything® Easy Fitness Book
Everything® Fishing Book
Everything® Krav Maga for Fitness Book
Everything® Running Book, 2nd Ed.

TRAVEL

Everything® Family Guide to Coastal Florida
Everything® Family Guide to Cruise Vacations
Everything® Family Guide to Hawaii
Everything® Family Guide to Las Vegas, 2nd Ed.
Everything® Family Guide to Mexico
Everything® Family Guide to New England, 2nd Ed.
Everything® Family Guide to New York City, 3rd Ed.
Everything® Family Guide to RV Travel & Campgrounds
Everything® Family Guide to the Caribbean
Everything® Family Guide to the Disneyland® Resort, California
     Adventure®, Universal Studios®, and the Anaheim
     Area, 2nd Ed.
Everything® Family Guide to the Walt Disney World Resort®,
     Universal Studios®, and Greater Orlando, 5th Ed.
Everything® Family Guide to Timeshares
Everything® Family Guide to Washington D.C., 2nd Ed.

WEDDINGS

Everything® Bachelorette Party Book, $9.95
Everything® Bridesmaid Book, $9.95
Everything® Destination Wedding Book
Everything® Father of the Bride Book, $9.95
Everything® Groom Book, $9.95
Everything® Mother of the Bride Book, $9.95
Everything® Outdoor Wedding Book
Everything® Wedding Book, 3rd Ed.
Everything® Wedding Checklist, $9.95
Everything® Wedding Etiquette Book, $9.95
Everything® Wedding Organizer, 2nd Ed., $16.95
Everything® Wedding Shower Book, $9.95
Everything® Wedding Vows Book, $9.95
Everything® Wedding Workout Book
Everything® Weddings on a Budget Book, 2nd Ed., $9.95

WRITING

Everything® Creative Writing Book
Everything® Get Published Book, 2nd Ed.
Everything® Grammar and Style Book, 2nd Ed.
Everything® Guide to Magazine Writing
Everything® Guide to Writing a Book Proposal
Everything® Guide to Writing a Novel
Everything® Guide to Writing Children's Books
Everything® Guide to Writing Copy
Everything® Guide to Writing Graphic Novels
Everything® Guide to Writing Research Papers
Everything® Improve Your Writing Book, 2nd Ed.
Everything® Writing Poetry Book